The Apology
A Blackman's Contrition to his Sisters

Second Edition

ELUHIM B. SIDDHA

The Apology: A Blackman's Contrition to His Sisters

Written and created by: Eluhim B. Siddha
Editor: Jill Duska with Devoe Publications
Interior Design: Donna Osborn Clark with Creations By Donna/Devoe Publications
ISBN-13-9781709474965
Published by: Eluhim B. Siddha

Table of Contents

Part IV: Embracing Love & Healing

Introduction

The story behind The Apology

Officer C. Brown. She was a correctional officer in a maximum security prison where she had to interact with approximately 1200 male inmates on a daily bases. I was one of those inmates. So one day when I paid her a compliment, telling her that she was a beautiful woman, her response wasn't receptive. She figured I was just another convict flirting and trying to manipulate her by prying on her insecurities.

She said to me, "I know I am not beautiful, in fact I am ugly and my children's father reminds me of it everyday". I then asked, "So no one has ever told you that you are beautiful?' Not your father, uncles, no one?" She replied, "No one has ever called me beautiful not even my father, he also use to call me ugly, so please stop trying to run game on me. What is it that you want?" I responded, "I just wanted to tell you how beautiful of a woman I think you are. This is something you should already know. I'm sorry that you don't think so. Have a good night…..beautiful".

Later on that night I couldn't sleep thinking of how sad her life must have been to walk this earth thinking you're ugly and being told so constantly. I was sad for her, genuinely sad so I began to write her a poem and when I completed it I titled it The Apology:

I solemnly apologize for all the guys
who failed to realize, honor, and recognize, the sunrise in your eyes.
I apologize for the men

who failed to be your friend,

before trying to be your lover – never to discover heaven in your mind, the wealth-like gold in your soul and all that's worthwhile in your smile...

And I apologize for being a child (in a child's place) when you needed us to be men, for not being righteous and giving into sin, and for not seeing you as that soul-sister, respecting you like family, blood, or a distant kin, and failing to realize that without the Blackwoman, Blackmen can't win....

At that time I was a young 28 year old male who had been in prison for 10 years so far with 5 more years left before my release. Everything I knew about women was limited to an 18 year old mind, from growing up with a sister, female cousins and being raised by strong and weak women and watching their journeys. From watching the village and the products of our environment. In prison through books, music and poetry I was introduced to Maya Angelou, Terry MacMillian, Iyanla Vanzant, bell hooks, Alice Walker (my momma), Sonia Sanchez, Toni Morrison, Sister Soldier, Asha Bandele, Jessica Care Moore, Eyrakah Badu, Lauryn Hill, Jill Scott, Angie Stone, just to name a few sisters and elders who had broaden the scope of my limited 18 year old frame of reference and understanding about women. Nevertheless, I had no hands on experience with women as a man and therefore little did I know or understand that my mind at 28 and even at 32, (5 years later) what I learned from these matriarchal legends would still be digested like milk, from the mind of an infant and not like meat processed in the mind of a man.

I was a relationship illiterate. Emotionally retarded and still an inexperienced immature male at 32 years old. I was caged as a boy and released as a boy unbeknownst to myself. I believed my teenage years role-playing as a man, having manly responsibilities, engaged in adult activities, surviving the experience of incarceration (rites-of-passage) and my intensive book knowledge was my right to manhood. Nope. Reading and having knowledge is not and no where close to having experience and wisdom. Being free was now my opportunity to apply everything I had read and learned but because I already thought I knew it all, knowing it all would become the cause of my downfall… but that's another story for another book.

Eight years later since the 1st edition of The Apology a 2nd edition has become way overdue as I have experienced what I thought I knew, lived what I thought I could never live. Enjoyed relationships, endured pain, shame, frustration, happiness, love, redemption, failure, and redemption over and over again. Also since the 1st edition of The Apology the experiences of Black women have not changed much. Even though we see progress on many levels, pain still occurs, heartbreak still happens, loneliness is still present, and through it all Black women are still celebrated, honored and praise. Maybe not celebrated enough and therefore these poems are still needed in representation of her/your glory and story.

Why Black Women?

I am often asked why do I only write poems dedicated to black women. Are not all women in the world oppressed, degraded, disrespected, look down upon, lusted after, objectified, glorified, loved and hated? Are not all women great and deserving of praise?

My response is a quote from our Prince El-Hajj Malik El-Shabazz better known as Malcolm X:

"The most disrespected person in America is the black woman. The most unprotected person in America is the black woman. The most neglected person in America is the black woman."

This quote found new life on *Beyonce's* acclaimed 2016 album titled *Lemonade*, where she also highlights the pain and triumphs manifested in black womanhood, their struggles and their greatness, their strength, successes and power.

In my response I also go further and state that the black woman is the most disrespected, most neglected and most unprotected woman in the *World, on the entire Planet.* Go to any continent and visit any country; Australia, Japan, Europe, South America, etc and the darkest of women are the most disrespected women, so much that it's a fact that many people are unaware that dark skin women even exist in these places as citizens or natives for they are not portrayed in the history books or media, in the magazines, commercials or tour guide brochures.

The irony of it all, is that the black woman is the most admired, imitated and lusted after of all women. Also, all women as do all men come from the womb of the black woman and therefore she deserves honor first and foremost. Of course one can argue this but the proof is in the pudding which is addressed in the following poems in this book.

So I write for my sisters first because they are my sisters and charity starts at home but also because she, the Black woman deserves all this overdue honor, praise and appreciation that I'm about to speak into her soul.

Peace,
Eluhim B.

Foreword

I met Eluhim at the *Jacob K. Javits Convention Center* in 2012 during the Annual *Circle Of Sisters* Event. He was a vendor during the event selling his book and preforming his poetry. Initially when I seen the title of his book boldly printed on a plain black cover, I said to myself, "I don't need an apology, I have a husband of 17 years who have been nothing but good to me". As I was about to say this to him another sister walked passed him in disgust saying. "I am tired of y'all apologizing, ain't nobody trying to hear that sh@#!" He smiled and politely stopped her and explained to her that the book is more than an apology. He explained that the poems in his book which he described as a labor of love, was an offering in honor of us (black women), and within the poems he is passionately expressing the triumphs of black women throughout past and present history. It's a love story of love and pain, hurt and healing and it's not the player pimp poetry aim to charm sisters out of their underwear. He had caught my attention further and piqued my curiosity. I stood there and read two poems from his book and was sold. Give me four of them I said.

Later that week I gifted The Apology to two co-workers, a close friend and my biological sister. They loved it and eventually we added it to our monthly book club discussion. Even as a happily married woman with no trauma or baggage that involved black men I still was able to relate, empathize and involve myself with many of the poems that spoke to my black womanhood.

Later on that year I received an EventBrite email invitation from Eluhim for his event called Poetry Over Dinner and another invite for The Divine Exchange where he and other artists perform their work and interact with the audience in Q & A and open discussion about the poems recited/read.

This was something I have never experienced before at an Open Mic or feature performance. The discussions were so open-hearted, honest, passionate, thoughtful and helpful. I called it a healing session. Sisters and brothers bared their souls and one day so did Eluhim.

At the last event I attended Eluhim spoke of infidelity in his marriage. The poems he recited was so raw, and shocking but the truthfulness of it opened up a discussion that was hard for many to have. I remember Eluhim saying,
"Often we think we are whole when we are not". That day I also for the first time opened up about some issues in my own marriage that was being suppressed.

After that last event I would often witness Eluhim tell people that he is putting The Apology on the shelf until he gets it right. I would comment "Brother, we need that book. Hurry up and get it right".Well, here we are now with the 2nd edition of The Apology, him with a new wife and a 2 year old daughter and an 8 year daughter from his wife's previous marriage. 3 women in his kingdom. I guess he is getting it right. He better.

This is not a book about perfection but it can definitely be added to the library of books helping us make it back there; perfection that is.
I thank Eluhim for letting me be apart of his journey; his open-book experience. Never hiding who he is, has helped me to also experience the healing power of exposure. This labor of love of his has also been a pleasure to have, to read, re-read, reference and share with my circle.

To my sisters I love you tremendously, we are about to take the world by storm. To my brothers we got you. We know you got us.

Faith, Peace & Love,
Assata Uni North

For the women that have inspired, motivated, nurtured and encouraged me throughout my life; Wife, Mother(s), Grandmothers, Sisters, Cousins, Nieces, Friends, all who have contributed to my growth, development and understanding of who they are and all that they can be.

Part I: The Phenomenal Woman: Her Strength, Honor and Legacy

...Ain't I a Woman

The Black Woman

So beautiful, pure and Divine
Where else on the Earth can
we find…a woman of your
esteem: sensitive, sweet,
sometimes mean
but always…always strong
under pressure, whether it's
slavery, civil rights, tribal
fights, or man-less nights,
you possess the might
of our great ancestors…
Loving gestures
you never fail to show…
demonstrate compassion to
those who don't know…
like the men who come and go
and still you grow, you grow
through all the madness
the sadness of it all…is
that they say, you, Black Eve
are the cause of man's fall,
but we know that
if a Black man stands tall..
it's because you are his backbone…
when he isn't home…you

uphold the house alone
control your zone it's known
throughout the world that
you are the Mother of all,
have a long list of
accomplishments, all great,
none small…And Blackwoman,
your honors are way overdue
your eyes, your smile, the
complexion of your hue.
In your face are reflections
of a world that's brand new,
refined and beautiful,
attractive and appealing,
your presence is a healing.
A Black Queen
restoring her crown,
for even though it's a man's
world, you, Blackwoman, make
the World go around.

Black Sister Queen

Blackwoman, I got a love jones
for your melanin skin-tone…
you're home-grown…not
artificial/official, no
preservatives or additives
bring life into proper perspective,
no longer acting like savages… for
where would we be without you?
I'm realizing that it's all about you.
You have become my high…
can a grown man cry…be shy
in your presence? Your
essence being that dynamic…
I would panic without you,
search for you throughout the entire planet…
This is your world – you be woman, not girl,
be Queen, not princess - be intelligent, not senseless,
names like b*#+! and hoe, I'm against this… you're
not defenseless.
I'm here to protect your honor, your pride.
There were times men tried to impress you with rides…
with money - but it's funny because your love can't be
bought,
but must be sought
within the depths of your soul and your heart,
love you in whole, not just in part - not just in fractions

this natural attraction that I have for you
is a passion passing through my entire being,
internalizing my senses, my feelings,
my hearing, my smell, my taste, my seeing.
And now that I know what it means to respect you, Queen,
I'll never neglect you, Queen – I've seen the world through your eyes.
Heaven lies at your feet.
I love you, Blackwoman, allow me to repeat:
I love you, Blackwoman, and it's your love that I seek.

Changing My Belief System (2005)

I believe in Blackwomen,
Believe in their ability to conceive… new
ideas, revelations and utopic futures never
expected that it's in her nature to be
easily deceived or to deceive. Why they tell lies on Eve?
I believe that Blackwomen can procreate gods
even when she and her mate are at odds,
that angry passion will fashion aggressive black
politicians, birth hostile corporate takeovers,
the womb that produces that riotous mob,
passionate educators, for better education
for better careers and jobs.
I believe she got that creative energy
to produce a Black President with articulation like Kenny,
a voice like Martin, a vision like Malcolm,

to detect the real enemy.
I believe she got the chemistry to turn a negative into
a positive, like changing the music industry.
I believe the Blackwoman has a trick up her sleeve/lasted this long
through the pain and disease/can't take but so much sh#@, won't
no longer sit and just grieve/I know she's up to something, we just
to blind to perceive/I know that Blackwoman
has a trick up her sleeve.
I believe in Blackwomen; from my side she won't leave/she's
proven herself often/still standing by even when a brother is laid in
his coffin/ spooning us 44D when our ass gets to coughing/ and

my hard head
got my ass soften/ because Momma
don't play… I believe in the day
Blackwomen will run countries/feed all the hungry/move century
old mountains/find the youth-preserving fountain
and save the planet.
I believe she's dynamic
and can have a dynamic effect,
transform sin into something perfect
with her Holy demeanor/ purify the soul, and make the spirit cleaner. I
believe in her wisdom, her intuition/her ability to rise above
any condition/to re-incision/herself into the spine of Blackmen and
be his backbone/bring him back home/to re-invent his position. I
believe she brought us into this world (Mother of Civilization) And
I believe she can take us out (not loving her, that'll be
our damnation).
I believe she needs a vacation,
a cruise, dancing, spa, a show, a massage,
needs a break from the desert, tired of seeing a mirage.
People pretending they understand her pain,
calling her Black Queen, Nubian Sister, Black Butterfly,
Soul Sister, like they truly know her name insincere to
the claim of her true identity.
And I believe our identity lies in her spirit, is rooted in her womb,
I believe she's salvation and judgment day is coming soon.
I believe she's springtime in bloom/grooms the earth like

young girls decorating bedrooms…and I believe that that's her face in the moon.
I believe she's all we need.
Time for men to sit down and let the women lead/God's
greatest deed/if she can nurture the seed, she can untangle the weed/
and pled/on our behalf to God…
Blackwoman, I know it's been hard and
that's how I know that, you go hard.
Heaven is your backyard/let's go out back and
disregard/ the negative predictions within tarot cards…
because I believe that you're the future, all that we need in
the present/reminiscent of the past/without your comfort, we wouldn't last…

Let those that hate you
disbelieve and talk trash…
but in you I believe…
….I believe in you.

Black Woman

I've seen men carry you across the River Nile in style
and tamed the wild through civilization…
I've seen you play the role of Mother and Father when times got
harder, holding every position from the lowest to the highest
occupation… and education has been your profession.
Class has been in session since the start of history.
We were uncertain about our origins, confused about God's nature,
and it was you who tore apart the mystery…
you've been kissing me since birth,
what a pleasure, like the breast that first served as my wet-nurse,
and Earth would be vanity without your pleasure.
Men dig deep for your treasure and you embrace us in full measure
and you miraculously stand tall, head high, back straight, after
nine months of pressure.
You've served all of mankind through all ages and
time, from the greatest of us to the least…
Everyday, every night, I'm praying, saying, "God bless her,
God bless her, keep her pure and pleasant,
raise her above the clouds with the stars and crescent,
give her extra strength, length of days, so I can demonstrate my
appreciation of her value with gifts and presents…
And let her evolve to solve all the problems in this world."

In Honor of Your Beauty

Beautiful to my vision, the collision of
  my visual and your present position
And I view you in all your beauty, truly a wonder of the
world, distinct from all seven heavens' favorite creation
beauty in your menstruation
   beauty in your labor
with honor you carried untold loads of good and bad seeds,
that's why it's you we favor
No soul aborted, no child left behind
way before Hillary Clinton plagiarized your line
  brought so many flavors into existence, tribes, nations, and
races see your touch of love and beauty in Asian, Caucasian,
Hispanic, and Native faces traces of your blood
    in all inhabited places
And Good Gracious your spirit is so divine refined
throughout the time and ages
when your men be locked-up in cages you
  step on and perform on many stages
play many roles, go through many phases and it amazes me
that through it all you remain sane and beautiful.

I Appreciate

….Every thought about you
when I'm mad, upset, lonely
when I'm overwhelmed with joy
and only you can make me cry…
make me dream…
make me scream…
Make me call my mama after every drama
And then appreciate you even more
….Every moment with you
when we do dinner
do lunch… pack lunches…
do picnics…
and every minute pictured in your frame
Polaroid my image in your redroom
and develop
and duplicate
and procreate…
our assimilated images
….Every sight of you…
seeing you birthday-suited-down…
T-shirt and panties
or the all-cream wedding gown …cooking
at the stove standing at a pose or legs
closed refusing me some… …seeing you
raise children
seeing them reverently raise you

seeing you asleep, listening, reading,
exercising, driving, dancing, relaxing…
seeing you mad, upset, crying, screaming
    neck twisting head oscillating
tongue lashing, lips poked out
  hands on hips, calming down
laying down, opening up to my
    appreciation…
  …break-up to make up…
makeup to wake-up…
and we do breakfast…
and I appreciate you more.

That Voodoo That You Do

She's a wholistic healing/ so appealing/ to my soul/ mold/ my joints together when they fell apart/ rejuvenated the heart/ and made me flexible/ stretched, massaged, and cured my mind and made me an intellectual/ got on top of me, made the healing sexual/ gave a soothe textual feel to my spirit/ with her R&B lyrics/ and with her spiritual hymns in every pleasurable moan/ a reconciliation of sins vibrating through my bones/ All my wounds were assumed to be fatal/ but I was easily restored with that Motherly wisdom that I received in the cradle/ with folklore's and fables/ natural herbs and spices, served at the dinner table/ no modern gadgets or devices/ had an organic solution for my spiritual, mental, or physical crisis/ she embraced me into her orange slices/ which was the greatest healing of all/ all my pains, problems, worries and difficulties were calmed within her arms and between her walls/ Natural Juices/induces potency and reduces/ weakness and seduces/my innate divinity/ stimulating sacred energy/ from the beginning to the end of me/ making me whole, my soul chemistry... She's wholistic/kind of mystic/ no witch doctor, just simplistic/natural, earthly, so intrinsic/ to my earthly nature.... She's my wholistic healer.

The Soul of A Sister

It smells like a kitchen on Sunday,
steamed by fried rice, collard greens, sweet potato,
pineapple upside down, chicken; fried, barbecued, and baked
and at night, it's everything from Avon or cosmetic and
    hygiene from Macy's
  Suave like Intensive Care and pink – gel for hair
and it felt like leather belts,
cotton bras, silk panties and smooth skin
felt like the color of charcoal, the sound of the sun
    and the taste of the wind
   on my lips....
and it tasted like fish and hips and sweet spicy
sour-creamed dip and flavored lipstick Vaseline cheeks
    and it sounds wet like CK Infinity on your neck
and nail polish remover feels smoother than leather
   light like polyester
everything in your bathroom cabinet and on your bedroom dresser
to the morning breath, natural sweat after hot sex pre-maternal
bleed post-maternal feed
   your soul is so complex,
your internal assets are so, so heavenly, intangible
    reminiscent of things past and present
   and your soul is present whatever you approach
you leave an impression on
   every sound heard, every loving touch and
feeling, every smell, every taste and sight,

every phenomenon like day and night,
your every touch and feeling
everything about you, Soul sister,
past and present has been a healing.

Single Mother

They say you can't do what men do
raise a boy to be a man, strong like a
Bantu spiritually in tune like a Hindu
and still teach him how to cook up any menu
and defend you, whether he's small or tall
when you're man-less he's the best man to befriend you
and continue to represent the principles that are in you,
possessing qualities that are beneficial and essential for
survival for his arrival
into a world that will bend you
if your back ain't strong and
if you lack clear vision like a window
And no one knows what you've been through,
labor alone, there's so much that you are into,
Mother, teacher, secretary, organizer, daughter, student,
provider, all in one week and at your peak,
you're a Diva raising a god to praise The One God
You disciple with the tongue, discipline with the
rod Sensitive you are
but aggressive when it's time to love
hard They say you can't induce
the necessary masculinity, but
I think you've done a damn god job.

The Omnipresent Woman

You came and went, went and came/not like men who come and go... No!
You established a Legacy and left a name/a historical figure
...that all men know, so...
you came and went/sent descendants in your place/to delegate your power in representation of your race/with the grace of a Queen/you went and came back with a team/recruited from the womb of the universe, the universe you groomed/and bloomed a nation of duplication's/you healed and nursed our castrations/and induced in us explanations of Creation/and God/taught the Lord's word like Moses and SOJOURNER(ed) hard/to establish the TRUTH/tell no fiction like Mother Goose/like Mother Earth you produce the things that mankind can put to use/And the proof/is in the pudding (Ebonicnic-name) that chocolate flavor/savor the moment I must belabor the issue/her physical is extraordinary but mundanely superficial/yet her spirit is infinite the eternal birth expression of a Savior/You came and went, see you later/but never say goodbye/you may reverse a young man's game, but Blackwomen don't lie/and never ever die/and you went and came forever present immortal Soul. Behold! A story told/since times immemorial about your struggle to bleed and birth/to feed us first/and claim your turf/to spread your wealth and earn your worth/said, "Damn Ham's curse"/because you've been blessed/way before the stress/and nevertheless/you hold it down/with a smile or a frown/you hold it down/and been around/in every age/since the beginning stage/every page I turn in the history books/Look! there you are from the lowest to the highest grade/in 16 subdivided to 64 shades/from the Ebonic bionic sister to the one with AIDS/uneducated or vocational trade/from Eve/to what's conceived/in the 21st century African descent American made/ from your kente cloth to your Wall Street apparel...

through your time travel/when you were a Queen to Pharaoh/and now a Queen to me/you came and went/went and came/always remained/extravagant or plain/mostly sweet sometimes mean to me/but always around/and what I've found/in you is peace/release/relief and I know I've caused you grief/you went, you seemed deceased/but you came/your rejuvenation vacation was brief/no need for an apology/for now I understand Black cosmology/in tune with the philosophy/of life and death/the eternal breath/this is black psychology/that gives an intangible understanding which they call insane/you went and came/you was my first/the next, the last one and the worst/I've seen you in the maternity ward I've seen you in a hearse/and I loved you each time/in each rhyme/in each kiss/and what completes this/is when I was fetus/you were there and the when the Lord deletes this/physical features/will disappear/and you'll still be there/you'll still be there/You'll Still Be There/ You came and went/disappeared/and reappeared/went and came never left/exist in every breath/Mother of the Universe and Civilization….. from Birth to death.

Indigenous Beauty

And you're the Most Beautiful
since the BEGINNING OF DAYS…
there's nothing new about this/ what's brand new is this cultural foolishness/where your value has been lessened/ the fact that you're a blessing/ has been removed from the history lesson/and man is lost in a PATRIARCHAL MAZE…

This did not start with me, Blackwoman's performance in a white economy/or the Willie Lynch strategy for slavery/it was once upon a time,
long, long ago FAR, FAR, FAR AWAY…
how they blame the dirt on Eve/as if man's helper by nature was meant to deceive/a contradiction/in biblical fiction/why not blame the dirt on he that was made FROM CLAY…

Yes, beautiful, it started long ago/ and it took me a while, but now I know/ a sincere contrition I'm trying to show/repair the damage/be patient, if you're able to manage/love is no longer a GAME I PLAY…
I now see signs of your beauty in nature, in heightened degrees/like the ayah's in the Qur'an I read/in the moon, ocean, queen bees/and trees/ I ask you please/believe/in these/WORDS I SAY…

I take partial blame/in this whiteman's game/ to devalue women, to devalue me, my mind was trained/I ain't no Casanova, me and Romeo ain't never been friends, now I know my name/my mind's back in the Motherland and I'm HOME TO STAY…

there's no longer lust in my eyes/more concern with what's behind your eyes/so please take a chance and LOOK MY WAY…

I'm trying to make up for all of history, from the beginning of days, 'til the earth's no more/taking this opportunity to settle the score/ put you back in first place/this race/to restore all you were before/ making this political agenda address your glory on a campaign tour/state to state, shore to shore/have everything in nature praises you from the clouds in the sky that cry down rain about your pain to the springs evolving from the ocean floor/ and I'm sure/I shall never ever again see or treat/or speak/of you as anything less than what you are…

And you're the Most
Beautiful since the
Beginning Of Days……

Bronze Beauty

Fashioned by the mimics of the sun

Blowtorch in hand, goddess of fire forming you

according to divine desire. A preordained plan to have your

melanin increased and maintain luminosity, a glow that has

lasted for millenniums, statue as standard by ascetic loyalist

Shinning in times of darkness, ages of depression oppression

the repression of soul still remained whole with the feet of Jesus

and Greeks plagiarized your style

Aphrodite and the Madonna

and they debate about Mona Lisa's smile

as if they've never seen your dark full lips

stretched ear to ear in intense heat when making a child

and curse those who've violated that privacy

the secret of your golden genes your Motherland blood

your 90 degree temperature boiling water, daughter

of Ethiopia and Shaka's yellowish brown

semen from down Capetown born in the horn

with the yams, mango shaded in places

where there's Indian corn and your South American form

received that equatorial blessing seen in

all native artifacts, shaped and polished,

made-up without make-up, high-esteemed, because you know

you grow in places where struggle is ordained and

you remained a reflection of who, you and whatever stands

before your presentation showcased as a historical lesson

of traditional style forever nurtured

never tarnished by gangrene like pennies

and anyway, your seven senses make your

value way greater than one worth more than whole mints

and yes, you mirror the tin, but still have

a heart, for you're born from the earth, beating

its rhythm of life the heat from its core,

the nourishment from its canopy and every

element that emerges from your soul makes

you worth more than diamonds,

platinum, pearls, and gold. Your complexion

is a work of art, artistic perfection,

you're bright, smooth, warm, hard, enduring all forms

of pressure. You're that bronze beauty

and I swear I won't ever ever

tarnish your image.

Sweet Pigeon

I'm making Shaka Zulu Love
to my Ebony dove just because
she deserves a soldjah to shape and mold her
mold the fetus in her womb and groom
the man-child or queen-child underneath the moon,
sperm patent with history, the legacy of our ancestors
patent with the energy to take punitive measures
against the transgressors, the land possessors of
this foreign land and Motherland
take them back with unshackled hands
Putting some consciousness into my push and pull
take a dip in full inserting spiritual backbone
That spirit in my semen
no freak-like f@#king like the Westernized demon…
no treason against the soul
call upon all spirits from around the
globe, ancestors of new, ancestors of old.
Can't afford to freak or treat her like an animal
embody the spirit of Hannibal

and conquer Hellenic thought through the
teachings my father taught values brought
across the middle passage classic
information traditional sensations
run through my spine entering into my mind
and body… black like fertile soil, teeth white, broad nose,
hair knotty…
She gotta be the original woman, I gots to be the original
man natural and authentic, straight from the Motherland
expand her thinking on this stolen soil
In my Queen's womb a Dark Royal seed shall boil
because I be making Shaka Zulu love
to my Ebony dove.

Tar Baby
(Don't Hate Yourself, I love you)

A dose of melanin to the highest degree…

Deeply embedded like the pitch blackness of the ocean floor like

the inner core of our solar energy (the sun)…

Black-a-moor, what are you frowning for, you're the most favored

recipient of that solar chemistry…

you got to be kidding me… if you call it ugly,

distasteful or unattractive

Since the days of old your midnight skin has been a sight to

behold just recently has this world gotten cold

and confused…

misplaced honor, displaced and abused…

misused language "black-ass nigger", hostile and lewd in a

rude, aggressive mood…

And so it feels bad, but look in the world… 16 shades,

64 sub-divisions…

from the highest grade,

to the lowest melanic conditions…

and your decision to be beautiful should be based on

actual definitions…

of beauty, not warped concepts from inferior mentalities…

dying shades of pale fatalities…

of an albinic vs. Ebonic reality…

And you're the closet thing to the True Reality, Black as the

universe the first to walk the earth   no curse of Ham…

in high demand across the land…

the Blacker the Berry, the sweeter the juice…

the sweeter the cherry, more blackness produced and

reproduced… and you're the excuse…

for Blackmen - I mean blue-black,

dark purple, charcoal-brown men,

a Sidney Portier/Cisley Tyson blend… and in the end…

you might see white, but black is right, Black is tight…

a sight to behold since the days of old

by all sorts of men…

Don't hate your skin, God's perfect cosmetic blend

And I'll repeat it again and again…

…that Black is Beautiful…Black is beautiful

You are Beautiful, Black is in…

…Blackwoman/Black sister, love your skin like I do…

no caked-up make-up, just that natural black olive,

Black Berry Ebony hue.

28th

The first moon…
Couldn't come to soon
Young girl in bloom waste from the womb, like
an open wound colored dark like prunes
perfumes to cover the sweetness fumes padded
to the maximum hygienic groom…
just like that, kaboom!... all grown up
Attitude and moods
don't mean to be rude and exclude the
fellas from the prelude to womanhood
but that's their 28th day, their day,
stay out the way… the beginning
of suffering a simplistic pain
becomes more intense if not celebrated, looked at as gain
an access to wisdom and intuition a position to procreate,
cultivate an initiation into a legacy of fame
refused to be ashamed of the monthly stomach pains
and blood-spilled stains,
for God blessed the Earth with rain

suffering, and strain a sign for men and women
of understanding a universe expanding. If the seed is planted wisely
no waste for nine months blood clots into fleshly lumps
womanhood's transition to Motherhood and it's all good
the first man fashioned from a little mud
today the process entails a little blood
embryo migrating in a bloodbath of DNA
and thus the world is blessed with a feminine quality
can't imagine that being a curse from
eating from the forbidden tree
but I'm glad it ain't that bad…
just a few days out of the month in the year
and it's clear that it's a process of purification
the development of a breeding station
and I ain't mad…
you're an Angel still, pure and innocent
don't be ashamed of that monthly cycle 13
or 31, your life is vital
body in pain the price of womanhood gained

and we've come to honor your

situation understand your mood…

let's celebrate that day, wash clothes, clean your sheets

give you a bath and massage and cook your food…

listen to you bitch listen to you bitch

and I think that's how you've developed that switch…

…Oh thank God for that 28th day

Peach Fuzz

Already has a beard at 11yrs old,
but somebody is still going to love her.
Somebody is going to love her
Because she loves herself and
her Daddy taught her that happiness and love isn't,
never has been and never will be based on the hairs or lack of on her chin, head,
above her lip, or any other place.
I have two long hairs (he says) on my left nipple and gray hairs in my pubic
jungle and do you think I wear tank tops and get wax jobs
before sun bathing on the beach? Baby don't give a damn about what a woman or
man thinks about your physical appearance, just let it be made clear that you
won't be disrespected and if you're rejected it won't be based on bias perceptions
and the deceptions sold in Glamour trash/waste of paper magazines
Or by what you have or lack in your fitted jeans.
But if they don't like Queens, then they won't like you.
And that's ok. Somebody is going to love her because she was taught
to love herself first and thirst for no one else but the approval and comfort of her
own soul and one can only add to the gold which she holds within but none can
rob her or cause her will to bend and sin against herself
by having a low-self-esteem,
imaginary complexes or false perceptions of beauty.
It's not really a beard. Just a little peach fuzz
And without a doubt she jokes about it knowing she'll still be loved.
Because
She loves she

Wisdom

They say there's a face of a man in the moon, but I know it's a woman. No man has curves like that, sensuality or grace or pain/28 days and it rains/and still it shines and lights up the night and when she's full she gives birth to werewolves, brings out the beast in man and only the flexible hips of a woman can shape a crescent and raise tidal waves and cause collisions, turning heads at intersections, and every time you look up out the window she's always there, she's still there, like the black woman never going nowhere, face in the moon, pain in the moon, teardrops in her crevasses – the source of all life, man on the moon looking for life? Look at your wife. Kiss the moon, them thick lips. broad nose, high cheeks, coarse hair surrounded by stars, alone with company in a vast universe misunderstood as a dead planet living way before primordial man and still stands isolated, independent, self-sufficient, naked tribal sister, a vision in the dark/the vision of my heart/in a monogamous intercourse, whereas other galaxies have many moons polygamous cycles. Her solo shine/after solar time/lunar groomer/9 moons baby boomer/and I see her face in the moon, they're one and the same, moon and woman, woman in the moon.

Progressive Uniqueness

You're like no other

after all that Aunt Jemima drama,

you still came through as Queen Supreme

we seen you rise then fall, then rise again

through all the misrepresentation, stereotyping

and the white-blend trend ….

And your men would sin

and sin some more with white women

And they imitate you more than you imitate them

because you somehow intuitively innately know

that she came from you your beauty so true

And they're only glimpsing you through

an abstracting view

never knowing all that you are in-depth

your Soul so deep spirit and mind your black-sun-baking shine

rewind back to the beginning of time

when tadpoles were still evolving from water puddles

and your struggle

was simply straightening your back

tall and erect, elongated neck,

head held high

way before the days of the hyena's laugh

and the Eagles cry of claiming continents…

When the world was yours,

Only yours, in tune with God

and nature, your womanhood

the earth would compliment…

there were no opposites

You were equal to all

and the dishonor of that

is the reason for the fall

of mankind and in time

as we explain that

we can regain back

the honor way overdue

what we've forgotten about you

what we'll remember about you

What is needed still like no other

No other is like you.

The Concerns of A Business Woman

She's an entrepreneur/I knew her/as Ms. Thang, Ms. Know It All/'cause she had it all and knew it all/wouldn't let me call/unless I made over 40,000 a year/change my associates, obtain some influential peers/and get over my fears… of success/and to stop blaming the whiteman/she asked, "What are your future plans/do you own some property, a home, some land?/I'm not impressed that your car cost 30 grand."/She asked to see my hands/checked my nails, my ears and neck, not once did she eyeball the crotch of my pants/Asked if I knew my history, my heritage, my roots/asked could I wear a Kente cloth suit/and trade in my Tim Boots/Asked me if I had any business sense/did I preserve any of my innocence?/'Cause/she wants to experience a puppy love/and rise above/that fast and freakish mentality/the immorality of the past five generations/she was talking about reparations and compensations/for the atrocities against the dark-skin nation/Asked me for my explanation/of Love and War, and God/she confessed that most men took her as being odd/they say she work to hard/have yet to win her over with flowers, jewelry, or Hallmark cards/they call her a bi-sexual intellectual/disguise her hate for men, by listing what she expects of you/but I knew her/Ms. Entrepreneur/won't ever settle for less/settle for our mess/She's a challenge, has high standards, she's tougher than leather/so I'm getting myself together/never say never/she's not beyond my reach or grasp/all I ask is for a chance/I'll do what I must, even if she demands that I have to sing and dance/because life is a lesson, a lesson indeed/and Mrs.Entrepreneur's a blessing, the type of blessing that a Blackman need.

"V"

Despising your V-shape is what makes
men label you as the cause of sin
and abuse your jewel, your pool of love
attracts so much hate. Your fate? No!
But why lie about your Queenship
your Motherhood, your governance of nature
and all that extends from the cosmos of formation?
Stars in your eyes, they create black holes,
jealous and afraid because the eyes intuitively know,
what's not exposed
the envy of a foreign enemy
abnormal and wasted energy
which can be used to honor you instead
decorate your bed
with rose petals and perfumes
bare-naked, no costume lingerie
masqueraded mascara illusions of who you are
and bathe you between intermissions
When will he see through his own eyes,

unconcerned about your breast size
and value what's between your thighs
value your spirit, the valley you've walked through,
the wilderness you've been in
and applaud that you remained firm and sisterly non-
threatening to his manhood, his so called vicegerency
and see that without the Valued-shape,
Victorious form, Voluptuous, Vulnerary,
Vulpine touch and Voluntary embrace, we be not
be gas-less testosterone tadpole seamen with no
intended destination. And that you're
not Vulgar, Vacuous, Venal or Vulturous,
but Virtuous in nature, Velvety in your
Variations of Vulva Vaginal Voodoo, and we be
not, be nothing without you.

Phoenix

Simple and Plain   Your Temple Your Domain,

the essentials to the game pure and non-profaned

can't re-invent you, no one is the same the reason why He came

why I come early if I'm done   feel no shame

for there's purpose in the aim, the abundance that is gained

in multiplying a legacy to remain

to represent you, beautiful, simple and plain

and no dictionary, no Encyclopedia can explain

in girlhood you train for womanhood, the strain to maintain

a healthy spirit, a mind that is sane

through a labor that's ordained, no man knows your pain,

`the weight on your shoulders, like months of rain

to dignified to complain

the intuition in your heart, the premonitions in your brain

give you insight into the future

that your efforts aren't in vain

womanhood is your claim to fame that glory is

evident in your frame

a figure of flame

Benu (Phoenix) is the name.

Storm of The Century

I was in a Soul Food Rib Joint where the walls stay greased… And
every waitress says, "God Bless You" whenever you sneeze… It
was then that she walked in through the door.
A strong wind followed, heels clicking against the diner
floor Maroon-colored autumn leaves brought in along with
the pleasant storm watch breeze
She speaks to Mrs. Chef, says, "What's going
on?" Mrs. Chef responds, "Child, please…
you know you got it going on."
Then the jukebox plays her favorite song,
"You Don't Know My Name" by Alicia Keys…
Outside I seen trees bowing at her knees
taken over by divine force/of course it's hard to
believe she had long African bangles as her sleeves
from her wrist up to her cut-up back arms sending alarms
through my homo-sapient shell…
spirit shaking, blown back from the wind
factor, 12 on the Beaufort scale…
136 miles per hour, rain, snow, and hail,

my head ringing like bells,
she moves so violently, so well so much force in her hips
my heart rips and aches
from her waist shake like an earthquake
and she finally takes a drink, her swallow floods the room
a sonic boom, the acoustics in her throat draws out the
night from the afternoon
sun setting before its time (to soon) hidden behind
Nimbostratus clouds and she whispers out loud,
"Can I have another drink?" and you would think
there would've been a warning…
for every man in the Soul Food Rib Joint came
storming… in stampede speed to buy her a drink in one
eye blink many tripped and fell in place
others stepping on backs, hands getting crushed,
footprints on the neck and face
they would never find out if her panties were cotton or
lace she had that much grace left so many men in agony
others left in amazement by such a divine like tragedy
All a part of nature I say

My mind catches up from its 20 second delay and replay

the moments, the whole event in slow motion

everyone drenched in sweat, wine spilled from broken glasses

hit by a wave from the ocean

and in all the commotion

she's unaffected her game perfected

roll through like thunder make all men wonder

lose a leg, lose an arm,

what a divine phenomenon

The price men pay to witness Angelic charm

she came and she went   was here and now gone

I'm satisfied with being the witness of such divine-like energy

Captured and swept away *by the storm of the century.*

Part II: The Pain and Ignorance

earth hurts….

True Story

{I hope she cheats on me with a basketball player......I deserve that karma.}

True Story......how I fell from glory

Turned into them dudes from Jerry Springer, Cheaters, Maury......

True Story I met this shorty who I thought had more grace/taste in the fine arts/an expressive heart/thuggish and divine/so fine and played the

side-chic part so well......

I fell... from glory, true story I wanted my cake and to eat it to/like eat her pussy and then go home and kiss my boo/the slime ball shit niggaz in the street do...

true story... spent time/with this dime/crossed the line/ when our souls did the rhythm and rhyme crime/and would break day blind to time/wine in my system so I paid wifey's complaints no mind

True Story

I've been judged in front of a jury....of her peers......

They say my words are bullshit/like the dude on the pulpit/who mixes bible verses with curses while eyeing sister Sonia/wishing he could bone her/ while his wife sits in the rear......

True Story.......now I'm like Oh God! oh dear/pleading/ because it feels like I have been barred from the Garden of Eden/seems like I just walked right out of heaven/and she's like You better call Tyron Dae Dae and Kevin!

Now I'm wondering how do I get back to divine status /because it matters/that no one can treat me like she do/true story she cooked my meals, washed my clothes/shaved my pubic hairs and clipped my toes/and now I'm out here in the cold unable to relate with hoes/lord knows I fell from Glory.

I use to be an Angel then I turned into demon/sharing my time sharing my semen/friends and family telling her you don't need him/he doesn't even... practice the things he writes about or says he believes in.....

LEEEEEEAVE HIM!

And she left me

Damn i know the way a nigga living was wack......

But you don't get a nigga back like that.......

I'm a nigga with pride you do shit like that.....

....,Oh well

Yes I fell from glory

True Story...

And now

The only thing that matters

Is that I get back to divine status.

Because I want to save my marriage / I want to increase her carrots/because now I got blinders on for the maggots that wants to fuck a man/whose wears a wedding-band /and I can....
I can   Do this.

Put me on a beach with freaks or amongst a colony of nudest
I can   do this

true story

All that matters is that I get back to divine status. To Glory

True Story

It Takes A Man 40 yrs to Get Over a Broken Heart

I could love you but....
...but it takes a man 40 years to get over a broken heart....
It takes a man 40 years with introverted tears to get over a broken heart

See I've been scarred and insecure since head-start
When I was getting parts
in my fade.....
And cared more about impressing you than
getting good grades...and you and Keisha threw me shade
Because my corny behind
drew hearts in cards
Instead of pushing you and
shoving you hard
in the hallways.

See that's some sh@#
my daddy was teaching at home
To shove a woman/Is to love a woman
To beat a woman/Is how you treat a woman

I didn't want to love like that/Like SuperFly or the Mack/like negros in the Trap/like fathers who leave and don't look back....
Like fathers who leave and don't look back.

See boys have broken hearts too

Men have scars too
We use to dream of rainbows, unicorns and stars too.....
believed in fairy-tales and happily ever afters....
until the teasing and the laughter
then shame
brought pain
and who wants to be hurt
by a skirt

So now we just flirt,
with your emotions
The little girl in you put this in motion
And I'm still healing, 40 years later from a broken heart.
You started this ish, way back in head-start.

Before I understood what
preference was.....
No light or dark skin
Short, tall, big girl or thin
Before I understood what
touching you does....
I just wanted to hold your hand, say we go together,
be your friend

But on the,
I love you do you love me, yes, no,
maybe so questionnaire

You left no reply

And now I don't care...

Now I'm a vain conceited bastard who likes Chics
with long weaves in their hair....
with broken hearts

COME BURN ME DOWN 4/20/13 2:45am

California Burning, willingly, calling the fire,
"Come Burn Me Down"!
With her native accent.
Not asking for a wedding gown,
Just come now
and
"Just Come Burn Me Down".
Come set my soul on fire
Because my man don't desire
nor can't afford this flame
Acting like the devil in the name of God.
Oh Father don't Burn her down,
save her from the fire
The Devil is a liar,
he says we can't get high off of
Your Love.
"Come Burn She Down". Without a sound
The smoke is silent but the spirit is screaming,
Smelling the flames, sweat, secretions and semen,
"Cum" "Burn" her "Down" says the demon
And her man is silently scheming,
A minute ago he was hoping and dreaming,
that they could spend a life together
free from the feigning
full of purpose and meaning
but in us there's a demon,

saying and screaming,
"Come Burn We Down".
Let's live under the influence,
Instead of Over the Influence,
Never Up, just Down
So high, but not Heaven Bound
And in her I've found,
the meaning of my confusion,
Why the forest burns,
but Bambi survives
Thumper's alive
and the birds still chirp
Because innocence is not lost
And I still have hope in her
even if my sanity is the cost.
I still have hope in her,
Lord please don't burn her down.

So Much Social Media

They met on Keek
A video chatting site
That same night
She showed him the kitten
He commented on how her
lips hanged loose
She admitted to her self-abuse
of having 22 (deuce-deuce)
sex partners since the age....
14 thru 18 now 19
Just looking for love on
her social network page....
He wonders how to address
this mess, if it's really his problem
or concern
Or just take his turn...

Mr. Right or Mr. Right Now.....
White Gown or Mr. Pipe Down....
Pleasure teaser of your taste, sight, sound.....
.or spirit pleaser, Heaven Bound.
Choose your poison, or choose your Healing.

.

Where's our Statue of Liberty

She was tall like Mount Rushmore - had all those manly features, European all up in her genes, (they were wearing bloomers then and still) an honest Abe and George Washing-them genes away, so now she's high yellow in the summer, close to red bone in the winter, with freedom of speech, freedom of the press, of religion and to vote, with no freedom to be Black like her Mother carved in Mount Kilimanjaro.

The Imperfect Place

Satin Lips pressed for time…

Steal a kiss hard-pressed pelvis

a quick slow grind…

Peeping around corners one eye open

the closed one focused on the intense feeling in

your mind… hands gripping your behind and

he says his best line… "I love you",

"You mean so much to me", "I want you so bad and need

you", "This was meant to be" and "I'll be gentle, I

know it's your first time"….

and he's so fine so hard to say "no" it comes out as a whisper,

and he pays it no mind

and touches you in places you've never been touched

G-spot in a clutch and the word no gets caught in

your throat and floats

back into your subconscious and

"oh yes!" is just a passionate expression

not an affirmation

no confirmation for entrance

Satin Lips pressed for time

trying to figure out how

to get out of this bind

it feels so good but the moment is so wrong
the imperfect place for your first taste

of the ultimate lust   rushed in haste

one eye open the closed one focused on the intense feeling…

so good   but the timing so bad

and possibly the wrong host

a foreign entity entering your essence

no protective garment and you

kind of   sort of   doubt

the sincerity claimed in his heart

legs begin to part   skirt raises

sensitive talk and sweet praises

both eyes close   never thought you'd be

making love in your clothes and the

word "no" is at the bottom of your feet,

ready to run… but you've been risen

in the air legs around hips

Satin Lips softly pierced cotton tip strongly piercing
the beast meets the yeast, no grease

no lubricant, no commitment, no romance
never planned, happened by chance
5 minutes, glad he's no longer in it,
it felt good but you feel bad sweaty
sticky whorish and wondering do he
still love you   or did he ever?

The Danger of Bed Strangers

Blood strangers/Bed changers/no engagers/for commitment/the resentment/from lack of proper affection/love's neglect-ion/and then stop caring/child-bearing/no sharing responsibility/emotional instability/don't give a f@#k/just wanna f@#k/no loving, just escape/morality declining at a speedy rate/a devil's trait/a lust so great/no feelings involved/can't seem to evolve/pass the first impression/eyes undressing/first night hands caressing/pelvises pressing/no confessing of love/no Lifestyle hats no Trojan glove/injection of an infectious mentality/insanity killing LUV/STD is **S**ense **T**hat **D**ie/ feelings gone out to dry/no perception/or emotional reflection/who transmitted that mental disease/just want to be pleased/love not a concern/burn and get burned/never learn last names/sex games/with no shame/no foreplay/no saving that for the right day/lay down with no ground rules/whose rules are these, who are we imitating/eliminating our race/hastening to our own destruction/reproduction at a decline or can't find the real father/why bother/negro ain't no good/neighborhood full of dogs, bitches, pussy cats and rats/so many players whose next to pitch, whose next to catch/contract an itch/which clinic/can we get to in 10 minutes/for pills/shots, abortions, a portion of a generation so ill/laying so still/somebody's dead/bed-disease/from Earth they leave/neglected the opportunity to believe/this wisdom: "Be careful who you choose to do the tangle/you just might be entertaining an Angel"... of Death.

Sleeping Beauty

You say I'm only good to you when I'm asleep
knocked-out dead on your bosom
… you put it on me like that…
You say, that's the only time you are sure of where I'm
at… when I'm asleep, dreaming, drained of all my semen
and you only receive meaning from me
in my sleep while I'm dreaming…
holding me, rubbing my head, exhausted, stuck to the bed
quiet, the only time you trust me
and the relationship is real…
and what happened prior to that was
just something to physically feel…
…but when I'm dreaming you see me for who I am the man
not the boy the child
the innocence not the menace
Inactivity allows me to be viewed in clear simplicity
and when I dream I ain't got to hear your mouth
you ain't got to hear my lies
all the truth comes out when I close my eyes

talking in my sleep and sometimes I gets deep and

express how I really feel…

…my fear, my failures, what I hate about myself, my

past, my present, my desire to heal…

And this is the only time that I’m good to you

And you wish I would just remain asleep.

Change The Pain

They couldn't begin as friends nor on the basis of respect/Approaching each other with a fake smile and grin/being evasive and indirect/about the anticipation, he knowing what to expect/by her dress and conversation/she knowing what's next by his lustful concentration/on her breasts and thighs/never looking in her eyes/never looking "in" his, never seeing each other/as ethnic sister and tribal brother/they see no relation, so there's no relationship/one or two stars in their little black books, 7 digits just a number/like prisoner's identification, makes me wonder/if they had the same last names/ would they still play the fast game/come, came, and go/could they elevate on high and re-descend from the low/and get to know/know thyself through understanding each other first/siblings of the same Mother Earth/Fathered by One Universe/and thirst for love/and now they see each other as One from above/Ebony Sister, Charcoal Brother, or recessive shades, kin before lovers/friends before the sheets and covers/related/in an elevated position/where they unite and are conditioned/through need and want/no dog in heat, no dame to hunt/She can be his gateway to heaven, she can be his gateway to hell/he can be her cause to rise or the reason she fell.

Young Fun/Grown-Up Pain

She was pretty and young/ I was grimy and dumb/and all we could do was have fun/she didn't demand/more from me because I had no plans/Did her belly expand?/That was not my plan/No pills, no condoms, no maturity/no responsibility/but a possibility/of experience by mistake/a remake/ of ourselves; just a child/about to have a child/and she's full of smiles/a little in doubt/I'm full of worries, what's fatherhood all about/should I take the getaway route/I'm OUT/But the baby is still in/and I begin/a life of running, she begins a life of pain/ Negros ain't no good, they'll leave you wet in the rain/no coat, no hat, no umbrella/slick ole fella/sick young lady/dying in the rain, about to abort a baby/a fetus/good Jesus/what if Mary aborted you/Good God! I'm through/done with your miracles, you can bring life to the dead/but can't make our men commit to one bed/one woman and one child, so she's baptized in her pain/born again/not the child, but the bitch that hates men/and in the end/She's so pretty and grown/I'm so grimy, a rolling stone/we both just want to cum/all we can ever do is have fun.

Genocidal Mourn

I can see my sea-men sailing down the wrong canal

my seeds one out of 1 million out of 4 billion

tadpoles swimming through the wrong women

planted and rooted into the wrong womb…

…to soon… premature relationships,

premature sperm 6 month term premature infant

in the palm of my hand This wasn't theplan,

a mistake from the start, a mistake in the end

the results of sin and lust so much vexation,

from a simple penetration… will it live, will it make it,

will Social Services take it, from the premature mother

and have it fostered by a sympathetic white woman

raised as a white child, with a white American mind…

Genocide is Genocide and in this day and time…

…it has taken on so many forms…

and I see no Savior so still I mourn,

like Dawn Still Mourning…. Still Dark.

Bestial Behavior

During the times when I was chasing waterfalls...

Brought the streets under our cotton

sheets and placed you on all fours…

…like four paws and I know you like it like that sometimes

but that's not divine   no love from behind   just f@#king..

it's o.k. sometimes   when we're in a freaky state of mind…

but you're no freak

and I should've never talked about our business in the street

for now,   my boys be doing it with your girls so tell your girls

I apologize and tell your girls to be ladies and women and

I'll tell my boys to be gentlemen   and men, let's set an example

for them   and try to transcend   bestiality

You're not a bitch; I'm not a dog…

I'm not a rooster, you're not a

chicken we're not monkeys, goats, or

hogs… our intercourse has to meet

reality so again let's transcend that

bestiality and be human beings

Moral agents of The All Eye Seeing

Incomplete Congratulations

She was my… what you call it? Soulmate

But I realized it to late   it was so late

By the time I realized she was my sunrise   -she was married, had children, we had separate lives -- but we still locked eyes   and we communicated so much in the stare, in the glance   knowing there'd be no chance   to really talk, couldn't risk that walk   around the corner, no private discussions about the past, or what ifs… or I should've and I apologize… Sorry don't mend hearts; don't restore the present or secure the future   And she halfway loving someone else   and I'm halfway hating myself   because the older child looks like me and if it is   she won't tell   and the man of the house is a good man, pays the bills, food on the table and treats her and the children well And like Vesta, I'm singing "Congratulations", looking for an explanation "It should've been me" time off from work, vacation, honeymooning

but that's life

my Soulmate another man's wife

Negros better stop playing freak in the street

before they go through life, with no match, no complement,

forever incomplete…

Sisters better get them Negros out the street

before you go through life, with no match, no complement,

forever incomplete

Natural

Imagine no Fashion

no styles no fads

no Macy's commercial ads no image to grab

to disguise your beauty

no tailored jeans to emphasize your booty

no discount no sales for press-on nails no

Asian inventions to deceive

with extensions or weaves no mental disease

with your natural appearance no interference

to Black Beauty with white perceptions no

light complexions from out of a bottle

no spraying hair with anti-atmosphere

and no push-up bras   drinks at bars

to mascara your scars

and just imagine you showed me you

and I fell in love with all of you

that natural actual you… just imagine

    this may be the key

        to me   being faithful and true

Be For-real It's the Sex Appeal

High-Stepping in high-heel shoes

Red color had me excited, highly enthused

which mack-line would I use

to catch your interest and keep you amused refrain

from looking like a fool and remain smooth

caught your eye, eye contact can't afford to lose

but can't help to keep my eyes off your boobs

mellowed-out off a little bit of booze high-spirited

tonight – I'll be the man you'll choose that boy

from school

a little childish still thinking sex before love is cool

no real intentions of marriage baby carriage doing

laundry and shopping for food

paying rent and car notes, joint accounts

and catering to your swinging moods

Money still tight like Jews enough for

one night, I'm still singing them lower-

class blues and it ain't no news that if

you've been used

I can't handle that baggage from the last savage
Keep picking the wrong men,
can't help if you're confused
Just trying to enjoy the night,
I'm giving you all the clues
letting you know, don't expect much
and there won't be much for you to lose
I can't change your man-hating views,
don't expect to be excused and exempt
from my mack-game moves
and short-term grooves as long as you
walk like that in them red high-heel shoes

Denim Behind

You took this fashion to another level
got your fabulous-ness from the ghetto
up-north style above the Mason-Dixon
fixin' to get Vogue be bold and redefine
Afrocentric sexual expression   fabric compressing
every part of your body
conform to your form
so often to close to porn
80% flesh revealed in your dress   and Lord
knows you've been blessed
with thick hips, thighs, buttocks, and breasts
and men of all races are most impressed
by a sister's behind and you look your best…
…in tight denim, Levis, Ralph, BabyPhat, Seven, and Guess
and I guess getting so much attention relieves social stress
Heads turn, tires burn,
60's era you said damn a perm
Afro-puffed with tight bell-
bottoms emphasizing your bottom

and you've always had a serious switch in your hips
an extreme talk in your walk, saying,
"look but don't touch" fill up them jeans
with so much and you done heard it all,
fries with that shake junk in your truck
dragging that wagon
must be Jell-O any room in them jeans for me
corny as some lines may be
the eyes can't deny what they see
like the gap in your Gaps
much attention you attract from the front or from the
back the view is abstract
like art and we drool like a fool
your disposition so cool when you're sporting them jeans
when it seems that the stitch
will bust at the seems   and the zipper in-between
as if you squeezed and you screamed just stepping in
catching sinful looks in them denims
and white women   is mimicking your style
Wow! You done took their fashion to another level.

No More Gluteus Maximus Actresses

Shake what your momma gave ya
Use what you got to get what you want
I ain't never liked those lines
about sistas' behinds.   And even when I was a schoolboy fool
grabbing ass in class it was never really about the flesh
just a test to see if opposites really do attract
and in fact   The Minister said,
"That's the filthiest part of the body"
the acquired taste of white men 'cause
they momma's ass is flat
the acquired taste of black men 'cause
he imitates how slave-masters act…
and ass is just ass
but her heart is essential, it's her spirit that will
last and if she has class, culture, intelligence
courage, spirit, and reverence for her Lord
she can be flat-chested, bald-headed, with no butt
just have a dowry that I can afford,
not like a Navigator more like a Taurus Ford
just let me get my money right
and you can get what you want without using what you got
all I ask for, is that you keep my coffee dark and hot cook
spicy soups, no pork in the pot and if my head hurts make
it stop
and I got you   keep what you got
it doesn't take a shake to reach my heart

Dance 4 Dollars

Front-stage-center in the spotlight
first night stage fright by the second
year she's all right cocky, confident-arrogance
don't give a damn and paid
A bank account, a baby fed, a paid tuition fee
no more debts, her reparations for a messed-up history
her affirmative action, proactive behavior
towards reactive circumstances yeah, she dances
she under-weighed her options, "so little chances"
that was a miscalculation a weak evaluation of
the overall social-economic situation
a decision that evolved out of hopelessness, pain,
and confusion relationships that were abusing
using survival skills to pay the bills
reason and intellect suppressed for a fat check
sophisticated disposition overrated because
it's not really a careerand I fear
that she'll get trapped
trick a little and don't look back
5,000 dollars a week the job market can't compete
so it seems what's next magazines
porn video scenes images for a young boy's dreams
and she'll say she'd tried to keep it clean
extreme measures to suppress them hunger
pains how long will she last genie in the glass
fulfilling wishes for riches call it success

but soulless   Any ones guess if she'll ever settle for less
or choose an alternative measure   aim for spiritual treasures
and fight worldly pressures   and fix this mess
Bless the child that has its own
but watch out, Mommy, how you maintain home
what siblings will contemplate in discussion about
you   once they get grown
not remembering those hunger pain groans
but ashamed of the name that came…
…from your flesh in the spotlight   local porno circuit fame
an ugly loan   borrowed from the world
that shouldn't be exposed   or shown
to children sheltered at home
now over exposed Mommy called…
…slut   freak   bitches and hoes
held by a leash chained to a collar walked
and curbed by that Almighty Dollar.

Premonition to Play with Boys

You let me dip my fingers and wet my beak
breast-stroked me, threw me up and defecated me
out, never allowed me in, past your shield through
the toll-booth immature in my youth intuition
revealed the truth that the boy will leave
the man wouldn't grow the child would never know…
…its daddy and that premonition secured your soul
from age-old pain, pimp game and
your first child having your maiden name
fortified yourself against sea-men
sailing/swimming through your peaceful canal
protected by the best protection
no Norplant or diaphragm erupted by your hand
running down your face and I called you freaky No!
You were really sneaky protecting your womb from
my plantation mentality
Slave master won't kill your child, you know the
plan Willy Lynch in our DNA
a syndrome that you're not bringing home
and so you never allowed me to reach your
core sucked me in then spitted me out I was
sure you were a whore
but you were saving yourself salvation
for your child to have a father, be raised
by woman and man, born into wedlock,
shown love from the

beginning to the end before and beyond
but you knew I'd be gone
and cause harm and you just gave
me a little   knowing I'd never give a lot.

JUSTIFIED HOMOCIDE

(The one who didn't get caught)

Been pushing pain/in your heart and brain/for to long/strong you are/star fallen has yet to be your fate/straight up in the night sky/high and bright you still reside/bride of The Almighty/Aphrodite Princess/and it's so senseless/how I treat you/beat you emotionally/no devotion in me/verbal abuse/loose with other women/winning with them but losing your trust/like a cruising tour bus/never home/roam the streets/meet all sorts of people/unequal to your glory/telling them your story/like they understand our pain/cock and aim/came home/you target practicing on picture cut-outs of my dome/phone unplug/hug me not/got gun in hand/demand my whereabouts/shout and scream/mean faces/traces of hate and disgust on your eyebrows/bowels loose, peeing down my leg/beg and plead I won't dare/scared to speak/weak in my knees/watching you squeeze/ease your pain/brain splattered on the wall/all your tears dried up/disrupt your glory and begin your fall.

The Conviction of Pain

I seen you bracing yourself in an offensive stance/adjusting yourself for violence not romance/preparing your mind/for doing time/in a woman's prison/like the decision/was so simple/ready to pop me like a pimple/for violating your trust, our bed, our castle, our temple/Frying pan in hand/ready to swing it at your man/your boy/played your emotions like a cheap flea market toy/contemplating smashing in my head/to bed/for good/bye/how could I/was your reoccurring question/"I'm weak" was the answering suggestion/ I thought confessing the truth would set me free/But now you yelling, "Just let me be"/I make you sick/yelling, "Pack your bags quick"/I got ten minutes to flee/and I plea/ "Please forgive me, understand/I'm just a man/human/stop assuming/that I'm that strong against temptation"/weakness is my explanation/but you're fed up with excuses/say my 9 inch was yours, supposed to be exclusive/for producing "our" children/but confusion/is all it produces/pain is all it induces/and I'm ducking your swinging fists/you ducking and pushing off my grabbing hugs and kisses/wishing you never loved me/How can you be such a fool again/dealing with these foolish men/where their desires keep ruling them/such a cruel gruesome sin/cursed with bad fortune/with a heart that lacks caution/and a portion/of your soul keeps getting stolen/rolling in pain/more lost than gain/pride is the cost of your shame/But shame on me, it's not your fault/I've been taught different.... Mama taught you to save it for love and/or marriage...

.... Papa taught me to play the field, to be a savage... not to
waste 5 months of my paycheck on a diamond carrot Mama
taught you that you gotta have it...the love and compassion
Papa taught me that if it looks good I gotta grab it...
just make love with passion,

keep girls coming back, or back to back/but he never warned me/that love would scorn me/nearly dead/bandaged in a hospital from feet to head/because my first, second, and third apology lacked a sincere repentance/three strikes I'm out, and you're in, doing time 10 to 25 year sentence… Damn, such a thin line…

Mirror On The Wall

When you look in the mirror do you see/What I see… do you see the butterflies in your eyes/and skies reflecting colorful sunsets and sweet spring waterfalls/in the gloss that laces your eyeballs… Do you see a Queen or do you think that's just some bullshit Blackmen say, a cliche, some psychobabble to boost your ego/Do you see that your ego needs no boosting up/you possess an innocence that no degree of immorality can interrupt/no shameful act can desecrate or corrupt… do you see that purity in yourself… the little girl in you, that grown-ass woman, the bad-ass, to fast, who was just so curious… about love, loving and through the storm developed an attitude that's so serious… When you look in the mirror is the woman looking back in fact mysterious… is she complicated and complex or is she simple like the young lady who wasn't old enough to put mascara on her pimples… and do you see your body as your temple… making men bow down at your feet… get nothing for cheap…. share your mind and body but none of it can they keep/Do you see the envy of other women who battle compete/and critic/your style/and all the while/smile in your face. Can you see your innocence calling you back/in order to attract Mr. Right and not Mr. Daddy Mack/Do you see the pain in your face disguised behind bright eyes/lies like "I'm okay." Lock up your heart for a better day… for a better person/right now just rehearsing/positions and cursing/God, wondering if He listens/Do you see the transition/from girl, lady/woman, tough, sweet, shady/intelligent, clever, confused crazy/what others perceive/but this man is not deceived/I see the true Angel that your parents conceived/and I'm pleased/with what I see in you/the woman you've become from all you've been through/and I knew/I'd fall in love from all your beauty and grace/I would've never looked into your beautiful face… and if you don't see what I see when you look in the mirror, your time in front of it is truly a waste.

FUNK!

She has Ham's curse in her purse/

Make-up to 'make up' for the beauty she think she lacks

swine on her eyes and lips, poison oozed in glued-in tracks

MAC her and pour her/Sephora dreams to disguise her BAre-Escentuals

and clog her pores to hide her sores and open up corporate doors....to be called a pretty mama. Commercialism's whore.

(Disclaimer: Not meant to offend anyone, especially those who use make-up simply to accentuate their naturally beautiful selves.)

I'd kiss you in the morning with your wake-up face

bad breath, cold in your eyes, midnight funk between your thighs

headscarf off, sweaty neck, passing gas, scratchy voice

with your wedgie and one sock off.

midnight funk between your thighs

headscarf off, sweaty neck, passing gas, scratchy voice

with your wedgie and one sock off.

i cOULD lOVe yOu WitH mY eYeS cLosEd....
bECAuse mY hEARts OPEN lIkE a WiDe nOSe....
STicKinG wITh iT lIKe a vOUge pOSe
aND LORD kNOws....that's how rEAL lOVe gOEs....

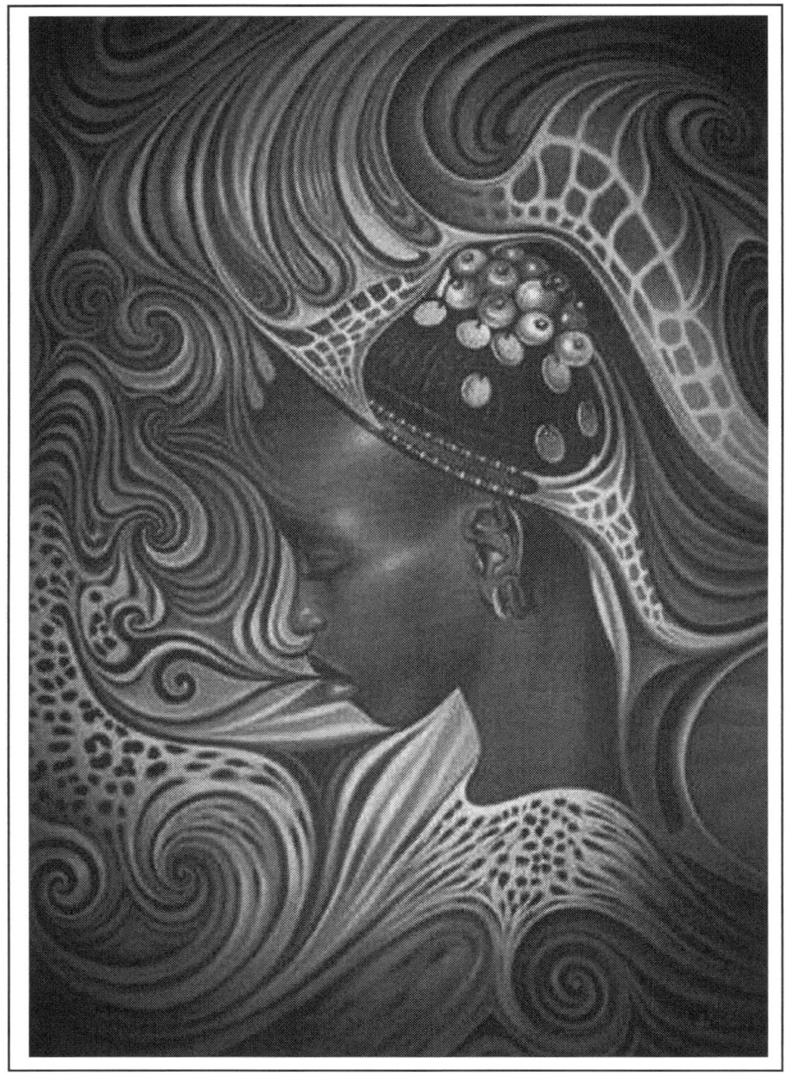

Part III: The Apology: The Future of Repentance

...and all that's worthwhile in your smile.

The Apology

I solemnly apologize for all the guys
who failed to realize, honor, and recognize,
the sunrise in your eyes.

I apologize for the men
who failed to be your friend,
before trying to be your lover – never to discover
heaven in your mind, the wealth-like gold in your soul
and all that's worthwhile in your smile…
And I apologize for being a child (in a child's place)
when you needed us to be men,
for not being righteous and giving into sin, and for
not seeing you as that soul-sister, respecting you
like family, blood, or a distant kin, and failing to
realize that without the Blackwoman,
Blackmen can't win.
And I apologize again,
from the beginning to the end of your pain,
for running game
and for the children we haven't claimed,
and for bringing shame to your name, being conceited and vain,
being involved with you, having no real purpose or aim… And
it's strange…
now that my mentality has changed,
I see you as I've never seen you before
the gateway to heavens door
more than one can explore – so adored,

because you're so deep, (I repeat) So deep!
And through your womanhood I've learned to be a man indeed.
And before I can proceed to succeed in this world,
I must treat you like a woman instead of a girl.
And so I apologize…
for failing to see the sunrise in your eyes,
because my perverted vision was locked on your breasts and
thighs. And now I compromise my lust for your trust and no more
lies in disguise of the truth.
And you are proof that God is good, God is Great.
And I know this honor is kind of late,
and my decision to express contrition is way overdue, but
Blackwoman, this is my sincere apology to you… …Stay
Black, Stay Strong, Stay Sweet, Divine and Beautiful.

No more Nonsense

I'm done playing games
and disguising my insecurities as macho-
ism, walking like a lion, but lying in my talk,
standing tall and erect, with defects in my planning
I'm done demanding what I'm unwilling to give
to live for you, stop talking about dying for you,
proclaiming forever,
but ain't got the present together

I'm done with just saying words just to be
heard, to calm your nerves, just to touch your
curves statements with no verbs,
no action, no message, no oils, no herbs,
I'm talking about healing, to rise from my ashes, emerge
with an emergency fulfill your lifelong urge with an urgency

I'm done with gifts with no substance,
photo picture frames, nicknames,
claims of my "only love" with a black book of my lovers
defining my manhood with no definition for what we have,
with slang absent from Webster's diction, i.e. my Boo, Bun,
Shorty, girl, old-lady, my baby and wifey, but yet no ring
I'm done running, on the run, sex for fun
feeling with no feelings, slow motions with no
emotions buying you flowers with no growth
buying you shoes, but walking nowhere with you,

down no path, no direction or destination buying
jewelry but the gesture being so un-rare,
valueless, no worth, being a curse
instead of a blessing, slick dressing
for no particular occasion
  you believing me with a little persuasion
because I constantly wear my best to catch the rest like I
    caught you

      I'm done with that
          I'm done

My Bad

I ain't got no excuse
I don't have an explanation
I do not have any justification
And it's so strange because it wasn't planned this way....
had no intentions, no desire
wasn't any benefit in making "pain" your heart's companion
tonight And what about those other nights
when the sun came up and pain was breakfast
companion, again and again, just like
my apologies... again and again
I'm sorry! "A sorry-ass Negro", you say.
But just listen...
It's not you, it's me
Heard it all before
But it is me... it's "my" bad
My bad living conditions
My bad employment situation
My bad social skills
...bad schooling
...bad upbringing
bad environment
bad association...
my bad history
history with women
history with relationships
history with commitment

history with love
history in America…
through the Middle Passage…
by way of the Motherland
and been motherless ever since
a slave ever since
a slave to my wants
a slave to my desires
a slave to my ego
a slave to my masculinity
a slave to my temper and to my fears
a slave to my ignorance
…but not enough to blame myself
for these hardships
my hard head
my hard heart
my hard fist
my hard private part
never private enough to be kept
hidden under the sheets…
its width and length not
a neighborhood secret
no secret that I've been weak
no secret that…
that nevertheless…
I still love you
need you… need you to understand
That…

it's my bad…
my bad ass
  my bad decisions with little thought
                with little consideration
    reactive behavior to things
externally pleasing to the eye
with little respect… for myself
And so I do us both a disservice
      and it's my bad
      my bad temper
      and those bad memories
of Mama's bad eye
perfectly fitted for Papa's knuckles
and every man afterwards
    no right to take it out on you
…. not   you…
no cycles to be repeated here
I won't do it again…
   not again…
you've done heard it all before
  but this isn't just my bad…
  this is my word.

Eye Wiping Clarity

Heart broken/all cried out and choking/hoping for a change/so strange that you can't find no man to treat you right/to be good to you in the day as good as he is at night/so many tears have blinded your sight... that you wouldn't be able to see Mr. Right if he stood before your eyes/in full size/no pretending no disguise/ with open arms/and all you'll remember is the harm/ that the gaming charm got you into last time/Negros faking love as America's greatest pastime, no more baseball, get to first base, second and third, home run, grown fun, childish ways/can't never regain the love experienced during them high school days/it's never like them Broadway plays/ no Westside Story/ no happy endings, no hope for glory/ no real beginning, because opening night is always a facade/ a mirage/ and you steadily dying in a Black "male" desert, cried out/Dried out in thirst/ "curse all black men" you yell/a choking inhale/never to exhale, release black males from this prison, hell-cell/in jail for our feminist crimes and selfish decisions, and we can't be released/ 'cause your pain won't cease to increase and come to peace/ just don't give us a piece and we won't become that beast/ instead of man/Hold out in demand/ that we establish some goals, sincere objectives and long term plans/ And I'm sure we'll get better if you mold us with your hands/no more heartbreaking, date-raping, attracted to just the hip shaking/no more lying, truth dying, patience trying or faking/if you're making...boys to be men/in the end/you can exhale/pay the bail/and from there together we can arrange/for a transformation in all our relations, no more choking... love is provoking a change.

I'm Chilling

Everything is cool now
I'm finally growing up
And now is when I need you most
To hold my hand - to have my back
and be the guardian of my heart
It's your investment, pumping love through my veins… for
you to heal your pains… they're through
bloodstream clean, a secure transfusion - life saving, nothing can
stunt my growth, to much energy and enough daily fiber to
excrete out all the bullsh@# and you supporting my back and
feeding me comfort at night, no longer skeptical about what the
morning will bring
and all the things promises bring, like spring… sure to come…
a definite… evident in my eyes
the new birth and good pumping evident in your thighs and lies
not a subject, it's an adolescent phobia, and I'm quite the adult now
Wow! I've finally caught up to you…
been chasing you since the library, always more mature, more
developed, more intelligent and sure… about your goals and
needs… I even quit the weed, you see my eyes ain't red with hell-
fire, now onto the Heaven in you that I admire and aspire
towards…

And Lord…
be my witness - we ain't got to do this no more
Everything is cool now.

My Responsibility

I can't even allow you to take partial blame
because I introduced you to this game
Secret love, both lustful gluttons,
I, selfish and greedy, wanting
my cake and eating it too
and you don't mind sharing daring to be bold
deep freeze your heart, so cold cold-blooded
and only I can bring you warmth even
if I leave in the evening
never stay until the morning
your friends call it whoring
you say, they just don't understand
hard to find a good man and good loving
and he gonna leave her soon anyway
Blinded by Dick-addiction, Hugging-Highs,
Cuddling-cravings, Tender-touching
and what can I say
this is just the game that we play I introduced it
The pain and confusion only I can reduce it.

Scream

This is no rap/ no lyrical soothing to play you into a Mack Trap/ to manipulate your emotional imbalance and get you bent over from the back/engaged in a balancing act/ In fact, this is a contract/ to move beyond, beyond way beyond the charm/that ends up being equivalent to the bullshit on dairy farms/part of a hen house, beyond those harems that produce nothing but emotional pain, physical harm/ I'm still screaming from all that pain/ that's what it is; a scream/ hollering out my shame, shouting to explain the mental change of a slave mind trained/ to stud you into breeding, conceiving ignorant images of my reproductive destructive caged-bird differed dream/ and I scream/out no more excuses, no more ya'mean (i.e. you know what I mean)/poetically purifying my genes/a DNA that screens out the negativity and spits out all that is clean/sperm so white, clear and translucent, a medium transparent/ of two parents/a spiritual transfusion, spiritual union, a Holy team/ This is no cheap rap, but a scream, an I'm-fed-up scream, a detoxing monkey on my back scream, a metamorphosis scream/ an extreme Apology scream, an orgasmic scream/Oh! Baby, Oh! Baby it's so, so good to be committed to the jewel you hold in between/ two thighs, two lives, syringe to the cotton vaccine/one love, One Lover, discover each other in the unison of the scream/ holler with me Oh! Baby, holler with me, Oh! baby, Yes! Yes!/got whelps on my back and chest/to brave to be a slave/breaking the chains/name is Kunta, not Toby/need my ancestors to know me/ won't let my predecessors forget me or the examples of brave Blackmen/to commit to one sister as lover & friend and transcend this slave-mentality of sexual engagements/with no diamond rings of engagement/going through the whole course/ of marriage then divorce/victimized by a society where adulterous actions is a ruling force/ my magazine of preference is no longer XXL, VIBE, KING or the SOURCE/but EBONY, "O" mag and ESSENCE/trying to learn your essence/and be a constant presence/ in your existence/fighting the slave mentality to be a stud with much resistance/with you in my corner, wiping the sweat from my brow, sponging water over my wounds, telling me I'm a winner, patting me on my back, pushing me into the ring, your drumming heart beating intoxicating confidence into my screaming spirit/ can you hear it/ no longer screaming from pain, but screaming exhilarating, rejuvenating, adrenaline pumping, rising from the dead screaming, screaming to get out, out into the world/ and tell my boys to love their girls. Owww!

A Plan

I'ma street clean the hood of Street Queens
make them a part of my street team, a street regime
to create a street dream   where the streets seem like sweet streams
where the streets won't be so mean
and the police don't come through with siren screams, high beams
and trees are green   detoxify the hood so the streets won't fiend, ya'mean
Lord, the things these streets done seen
Sister Soul supreme, I got better methods of getting cash and
cream, you ain't gotta be no Street Queen you ain't gotta be no
Street Queen
don't be fascinated by the diamond gleam
you don't have to take it to the extremes, acting past your age
only a teen
or not acting your age at all, where's the self-esteem,
the self-consciousness of the monstrous situation we're in
I'm crying in pain but no one's hearing
I'm fearing   that no one's caring
and that I face this task alone.

Love: A Transforming Power

What's going, sister?/Mister wanna know/I'm a man today/play
games no more… Kiss and tell, did I score? Telling males it's none of their
business… 411 is public information and we're not
listed… if I kissed it… no one will ever know
if you kissed it… it won't even show in my glow
Today I shine for you and radiate my heat/black tar & concrete
We can warm the earth, but keep it out the
street… 'cause nothing grows around toxic gas/
sidewalks trashed/ feelings masked/mouths run fast…
and the flesh is weak… where the phone line/is like the
clothesline…
I would never hang you out to dry in the concrete
jungle where boys lie… love dies and the meter
keeps ticking…
can't park love here/ a reserved space for touching and licking no talking,
no intimate, political or cultural conversation/ so where can I take you,
sister?/ Mister wants to know… a man with a plan/insistent to grow…
But do we go outside the hood/to make love any good
Or can we bring it back before all the innocence and consciousness gets
trampled/set examples of love
instead of lust/crush these skyscrapers/to many phallic symbols around to
many subliminal issues/need to be addressed… lower the dress… belt
buckles stay tight…
bring the meadow scenic/to this ghetto clinic/under the moonlight… Can
we do it together, you and me? Save love for you and me/like a true MC…
would save hip-hop/

hips locked/ a pair… A force to reckon with if you dare…
I got you, babe, that's Sunny and Clear…. In the sky
love birds fly… so we can't stay grounded Shaq and
Lil' Mo ain't Superhuman… if love ain't
blooming/assuming their adults… where are the mature
results… Let's end this/transcend this/ love is
endless/so why we ending… we ain't finished yet/the
white line hasn't been torn and nobody has received
trophies…

and in the night sky I see Sophie… let's summons this energy
and do our part I'm a man today, play games no more don't
pull hair and run… Pulling up my pants when I'm done no
more of that/matter of fact/matter factual…
I got exactly what you want/Sister, this Mister wants to know
what's it gonna be…
can we teach a young nation how to love exclusively?

The Genetic Curse
(Periods are unnatural)

I've metamorphosed into an exclamation mark!
standing erect, excited/but still benighted/by the
suggestions/in your curved questions/in the dark…
but I'm transforming Clark/into Superman/but darken up like the
Shaka from Zululand (minus the spandex) and I've leaped over
the tallest skyscraper towers…
exercising such powers/over any false phallic symbols/to move in
you/and through you for hours…
penetrating your strength/eliminating my weakness… stimulating
the length/of your canal to defeat this… this genocidal plot/shoot a
potential shot/into your womb/rejuvenated myself for nine months
in your embryonic cocoon/the most pleasant coma/the aroma/of
rhythm…
each comma a re-conjunction of two souls,
a transition towards politicalism…clearly/no theory/we possess this reality…
an apostrophic approach in quotation marks; Kings and Queens approach
towards Re-Africanization/ a full explanation/towards regaining identity… a
military manual on how to aim at the enemy…
covering health issues on eating the right foods, providing
nourishment for two/encouragement through you/and I/unison to
provide/a clean colon/that support, two marks: between the hours
and minutes of time I'm evolving behind a stomach that's
swollen…
and in month number nine/I've shined/like a trinity/the energy/of
hips moving/the fusion/of souls/what grows/is juxtaposed/with

flavor/a savior/is born/adorn and anoint…
and every joyful expression with an exclamation point…
evolving out of my shame/with a new name/re-identify self and re-define why I came/and the stitches come loose I come again,
a perpetual process/the progress/of multiplying/and satisfying/the earth/no blood lost, challenging the Edenic curse/birth/has no pain, has no end, my blood is repentance /never
ending the sentence/of life/enticed/by the natural feminine structure/puncture and re-puncture/the Queen of all land/ not the Queen of the Damned/bloodline existed before the construction
of the Pyramids…
never wasted in vain/runs through all of mankind's
veins/capitalizing your beginning/never ending/no periods…

Sisters Who Love Sisters

I don't know how, when, or where it started,
maybe with the individual self, isolated, legs parted,
curious, experimenting with self-love/satisfaction through finger action…
Don't mean to sound derogatory/but to question my own ignorance is sagaciously obligatory/trying to figure out the story/of the matriarchs who have turned their backs on Blackmen who sin/just to sin again with women friend/fed up with the droughts of mental, spiritual, emotional, and physical satisfaction… so opposites are no longer the attraction/and appreciation/is found in someone who can relate, a painful relation/yeah, "men ain't sh@#" becomes an explanation/ for same gender interaction…

….intercourse/where the touch is so, so soft/never forced/Who's the Boss/role-play or roles switch/who's the butch, who's the bitch/who's gonna bop, who's gonna switch/switch, switch the game around/from the pain that's found/in male-female relationships/fed-up with that bullsh@#/you say that no one knows a woman like a woman does/does a woman like a woman does/'cause each others needs are understood/and I'm just trying to understand, as if I can, as if I could/is it not my own fault again, my bad/because my performance and responsibility as a man has been sad/sad to say that some men don't min e the way you play/double standard, turned on by whom which you choose to lay/but got all bad things to say about boys who claim to be gay/and so I sit here today not judging you, judging you is to easy…

I just want to know if you can come on back/I'll pay more attention to your needs,
comb out your hair, communicate better, massage and caress your back

make a full effort to please you first, and this alone will please me…
I love sisters too/but I don't want to share you with you/bad enough I gotta compete with Whitey/and with the Dollar Almighty/corporate America, material things/and all the comforts that intoxication(s) brings/European Romance and R & B lyrics…
I'm not debating about right and wrong/but in my heart I know it's with me you belong/my soul tells me so/so don't ignore your spirit/man, woman, child/it's been flipped around, when, why or how/the origins are so mysterious…
Never mind the philosophical, psychological justifications/the scientific and biological explanations/the love is love rationale of heighten sensations, spiritual or moral or just a phase\fade of these past four generations/is it truth or dare, truth or a lie…
Engage me in this dialogue/about *The Vagina Monologue*/my mind is fogged/I know that a woman's love is so intense/and that we as men lack that intuitive sense/and so you
prefer girl over guy/sometimes bi-/or a complete boycott, penis-entry-denied/and you tell me you don't need or want me, looking me straight in the eye…
Now I'm feeling the same rejection you felt from me/alienated from your womanhood, experiencing jealously/knowing I can love and please you the way that she do/be more sensitive, tender, sincere and true/committed to you in divine unity…
I don't know how, when or where it started/but this future Father and Husband is brokenhearted/and I know your heart is closely guarded/ you're fed-up, disgusted, done with me, through with me/but I miss you so much

need your touch, by my side, in order to repair the family unit and restore the black community…
If you come back to me, please come on back
I'll make a promise to you, me and my boys will make a pack
…to love like sisters who love sisters… …and include true manhood with all of that.

Working On It

I don't know what you're thinking, what you want or what you need...
but I act like I do
And all that you reveal about yourself....
I act like I knew
And when we have a problem I act like it's your problem, that you're the problem that the situation can be solved with good sexual intercourse or a monetary exchange
disregard a verbal intercourse or an intellectual exchange
....I mean... I talk about change and being better
and getting through this together   and plans for tomorrow
but all the next day brings is sorrow   and pain
And it's because I don't understand you   more so
I don't understand me   Know that I possess quality
but quantity   of spirit   and deliberate
thought is lacking   attracting nothing but
negative vibes from you to me reciprocate back
and still I act like I know what's wrong
try my best to stroke in you deep and
long and even then my will isn't strong
try to learn from men who cry in their R&B
songs... ...like Keith Sweat
but that sensitive level I haven't reached yet
and you expect so much more from me to
conform to what's normal for a couple no
individuality, but a double
and I wish I really could read your mind and shovel...

…shovel away my own thoughts and misconceptions
and concealed deceptions of my ignorance and we
can think in line
and in time, I'll know what you're thinking
because in time, I'll really know what you're thinking.

Misconception

It's always been a physical thing
Never the major parts like the eyes and ears
and your brain... the ability to perceive, see,
listen, and comprehend...
It's always been your fingernails, hair, legs,
breasts, thighs, hips, and rear end...
Never accepted you when your presentation was plain
It's always been your walk file talk gold teeth...
short skirt and all that's underneath
Never meant to be the virginity thief...
It's always been about the physical for that's all I know
it seemed to be the ultimate result...
Never considered it a problem as a promiscuous boy
and enjoyed it even more as a freaky adult...
It's always been about looking sexy or having sexual potential...
Never knew the soul & spirit were essential and that
the mental was fundamental...
It's always been about your style, your fashion, your
material appearance...
Never thought your intellect or spirituality would cause
a stimulated interference...
But this is what you do when you choose to
make boys into men
extract the sacred from the perceived
sin turn niggas into gods
love into a job

and a spiritual experience…
It's always been about me
never been about you
but you've transformed my point of view
seen through the physical illusion
produced a spiritual union
and the conclusion is
that it should have always been all about you
and now it is

Labor & Delivery

At first
I was unprepared for it
it was to heavy for my heart
I'd rather be torn apart by spraying bullets
overdose on raw heroin and pure coke
and drink my kidneys apart
I never knew where to begin, how to start
reciprocating love back into your being
  never really seeing the healing
In the feeling the divinity in that
concept the serenity of life
All I'd seen was the price to be paid
     Unity delayed
Wouldn't give up being an individual
wouldn't be two-dimensional
one-sided view vision like an animal: black and white
no colors of love just functioning off of instincts
  And love was alien to my jungle nature to domesticated
  to relaxed to human to close to God and
  His loving Angels   and I didn't feel
    deserving of such salvation
  so I numbed my heart   and
manufactured a void of all sensations   and
disguised my escape as weaknesses towards
   temptations   when I was really just
to weak for a divine conception of pure emotion

And God loved
the world so much that He gave us you
but I refused my baptism no soulmate
no soul-healing promoting a life of division
many women like polytheism worthy of none
couldn't stand the pressure and the weight of
the Unity in One and then We had a Son
a holy trinity reflecting me
and reflecting you Damn!
Now what else can I do but genuinely,
no fighting it, courageously love you
For God loved the world so much
that He gave me you and salvation through
a child You made me born again Now…
I'm lover, husband, father, friend
and still I get afraid but I know
we'll win for love conquers all things
as it was in the beginning
So shall it be in the end

Bad Reception

Your love called me many times
Like an Evangelist converting me to your heart
And I so often refused salvation
To be baptized in your wet kisses
To be resurrected as your soulmate
And I always came to late - or to early Running
away when I didn't understand everlasting the
definition of love unable to see that far
Immortality being a childhood fantasy But loving
is quite grown-up
A growing that was incomprehensible to my young
mind Never been taught that Heaven can be on Earth
that we can be transformed into Angels
and fly above our fears, insecurities,
complexes and doubts…
is this what I've missed what love is all about…
And you kept calling me, and my heart kept
hanging up… bad reception
my receiver was not receiving love
or returning the call to love
- Bad reception - that's my excuse to
much static and automatic reactions
Like "I can't hear you", "there's a bad connection"
and eventually hang-up, close up and never call the company
that services such communications,
i.e. ***M***arriage ***C***ommitment ***I***mmortality, no wedding

Bells in the ***Atlantic*** no romantic cruising
on the ***Verizon*** where the sun sets
And I've been alone so long
No light on, no heat, disconnected
Can't receive your calls even if I wanted to
Living in emotional poverty in my own prison
captured in a cell
Unable to hold my head high
so it's hand held
And it's funny that now I can
hear you calling
I can hear you now
I'm coming over.

All That Disrespect

Remember the first time I disrespected you
As a father I said you wouldn't be sh@# beat
you with a switch (Post-Slavery Trauma) As
a boy I called you a bitch
And I accused you of being a gold-digger because
you wanted a man that was rich
I referred to you as bourgeoisie and proper-acting white wannabe
envied the fact that you waved your Ivy League degree in front of me
and when we were married I hated that you carried the majority of the load
Your job paid more money so you provided the heat when it was cold
and my heart got so cold
Released my stress on you, boss scream at me I scream at you
and when you wore your hair natural you was called nappy-head
called you light-skin bitch/dirty reds
took your virginity in a cum-stained bed…
…other sisters have been there before Remember
the first time you were called a whore
black-ass bitch, tar-baby, you ain't sh@#... black as sh@#
look at your clothes, your mama's poor
Was it I who introduced you to racism before white folks
did high-yellow girl called half-breed kid made you insecure
about your short hair
left you to fend for self at Parent Health Care
it's never been fair… all the disrespect
told you we'd always love you but never offered all that you'd expect
never approached you with my heart; always hard, hot, and erect

and you tried to keep me in check… with no win, all losses…
to many bad relationships, molested you as father, uncle, cousin, big brother
neighbor, friend, boyfriend, man, husband, pastors, teachers and bosses…
And it has cost us so much it's so hard for me now to reach your heart
ADT systems are keeping us apart
So much security protecting your soul   vacuum the black hole
but never sucked all the way in, and I'm cold
that's as far as I can go and never really know if I'm forgiven Now
I'm speaking to your pain, "Will I ever be forgiven"?
Shall you kill me in my sleep for treating you so cheap
or will you awaken me from this sleep so that I can begin and finish
living? For as long as you're in pain
I can never clear my name of shame
never make it up to you and claim a reward for my repentance
or a lenient judicial sentence…
…for my admittance and contrition and in addition… …to
my Apology
…I advice the psycho-analogy of he root of these painful issues
no more tear drop torn tissues
please allow me to wipe your eyes
kiss your teardrops, forever at your service… I
apologize… …no more disrespect, I apologize.

One More Chance

How do I get back right with you?
Reinstate my position within your heart…
Prevent this slow death tearing us apart
into two different people no longer equal
No longer living the same lifestyles now frowns
instead of smiles in each others presence while
others invade our presence …
…new cultures newmoney the situation has never been funny
So why have I never taken it seriously and
now I see you faded into the white the reflection that I fight
that which diluted my strength, my might my intellect, my sight
And I know what's right but it's all wrong
Me hanging long doesn't get me by no longer
Keep asking for honesty want to entrust your trust
Invest in my word to act on what's just and crush
all doubt about my intentions tired of clenching on
to promises, having no real faith in me
and I, having no faith in you acting unfaithfully
Am I getting what I deserve, what we deserve?
You say I have some nerve to offer an apology
Ask for forgiveness, for you to acknowledge me
On my knees at my most humble position, I beg and I plead
It's not to late; it can't be over turning your back on me
Gave me the cold shoulder the silent treatment
because now you have secrets
Private thoughts about our predicament

And you only use your mouth as an instrument to
cause an incident where we fuss and fight
Where it's a must you incite my guilty expressions
And suppressing your true feelings want me to stay
but tell me to go and I watch what I say keeping my
tone low, buying some time,
changing your mind convincing you to reconsider,
extract something sweet from a situation so bitter
I used to know how to make you smile but
now it takes a while looking through my
memory bank, every document and file
And finally it comes to me
All you ever wanted was to be loved,
appreciated and given attention
And all I ask for is an extension
…some time to get it right…
Now that I remember
I vow to get it right.

OH GIRL!

Those were the days when loving you was a challenge/and we'd manage/with puberty's lust/making out/French styling about/never getting to savage/never developing bad habits/like tongue kissing in public/and going all the way was a taboo subject/and even though we stimulated the physical parts/like caressing, stroking, fingering, and grabbing the behind - I had to
first stimulate the invisible - your heart/and caress your spirit, earn your trust and enter you through your mind/and it took time/like weeks or even months/before you would finally offer the remedy to rid me of puberty bumps/graduated beyond the denim-jean-grinds and zipper humps/no longer limited to stimulating each other with the hands/no longer restricted to getting wet underneath buckled pants/and it was love I felt/once we rewarded the chastity belt/love complete/like consummation confirmation that lust wouldn't destroy us, lust wouldn't defeat/and we did not internalize any kind of shame/we refused to have our pleasure involve any pain/never made you yell, holler, scratch, buck-up or scream my name/didn't play such games/we were relaxed/once we climaxed/and tears in your eyes were always tears of joy/a joyous cry that I treated you like a lady and that I was no longer a boy/And oh boy, them were the days/before the break-up, before our savage ways, before the emotional claim to pain/before the change/of morals and changing mates/before now, where everything happens on the first date/ except commitment Oh boy, I miss them days when you made me wait/and demanded commitment before love metamorphosed into hate/and received resentment And people say we can never go back, but I say we can/go back to long walks, modest hugging and holding hands/making commitments and making plans/and that's my plan, never was your

boyfriend, you were to grown for that, you called me your man/I didn't comprehend it as a demand/now I do, and that's my plan be
the man that you say I am/meet that challenge/fix the damage… be a man.

UNDERSTANDING

All this emotional activity, has me understanding you in degrees
30 below and my thoughts are on freeze
from a heart so cold –   you should have been told
that my mind has been diseased,
refrigerated germs not concern with your needs
Got pleasures to please   so much pain has been conceived
and so I'm stuck on that   -- frozen -- for I've chosen
this subject this fact
a consensus statistic   surveyed amongst blacks
where the mental temperature lacks a neutral warmth
and we're in danger if healing don't come soon
in doom from these complex feelings and problems
which originate in the womb
and I'm trying to groom   my sons   my boys
in preparation for what's to come   before
and after they come   to avoid
the pain and create the joy and destroy
the cycle that our enemies employ,
our complexes, insecurities, anxieties,
our pain, and the exploitation of our basic needs,
the capitalization of our demons; jealousy, lust
hate, envy and greed
Fashion my seeds with passionate pleads that
I've heard in your heart,
"Please be a daddy, need a man… provide for family,
satisfy desires, protect us from the Klan… do your part

start a business, travel to nice places… unite the races
resurrect the revolution   Blackman's solution
to Blackwomen problems."   Just be patient
those problems are new, lets get back to what's ancient,
embrace the original culture   abandon this criminal culture,
we've come to know in the West
test the old remedy   all innovation has failed
I'm chasing the tail   as it was in the beginning,
so shall it be in the end   forever friends,
like when I was in your womb… ummm…
all this emotional activity has me understanding you.

All That Glitters Isn't Gold

After all is said and done…
…you're the one… Oh God!
I have been aware of this fact…
but today it hit me hard… hit me so hard
nearly caused a heart attack…
heart didn't stop, but it was beating so fast…
an overdose of joy, ignited by our future and our
past… and at last… I feel complete
no longer do I seek what I've found in you,
have plans of surrounding you…
…with all that you need, giving all that I
have And after it's all said and done…
I'll still be loving you when we're 91…
old and gray and I'll be so bold to say…
…that I'll die for you… but I'd rather live
forever…
…this I'll try for you,
in order to make our love eternal…
beyond the physical turning you,
into something truly spiritual and earning you,
a position in a realm that's invisible;
a Heavenly Paradise Oh! Christ

I've done gambled all my life,
cost me nothing to roll the dice,
but for a Blackwoman's love I've paid the price,
sacrificed all that glitters but eventually turns
bitter and settled for the gold.

Malja

Sister, we got seeds to breed/feed a nation in need of liberation/I plants the idea in your souls incubator/the terminator we challenge/and manage without their birth control/to rob the soul/of fertilization/a castration plot by a frighten administration/of population growth, righteously they know us both/King and Queen/a supreme team/dominate gene/so they fear the excreting mixture of our souls/sweat drips from our head to toes/and what grows/¾ of a year later/raise 'em above the head in the night sky to the Creator/name 'em Yimic Malja, that means righteous liberator.

The Vision & Inspiration

I've wrestled with the Angel of Language to steal the right words,
"pure and divine" in which to express my soul's revelations… I've
reached deep into the ocean for every buried treasure, looking for
the rarest jewel to match my soul's sensation…
to offer them both a presentation a gift to your woman-nation,
to honor your creation, for whom would I be without you
as an explanation…
…to define my existence and resistance to elimination
All these genocidal plots; drugs, birth control, violence, and incarceration
and still I draw power from you for mental elevation, physical
emancipation, and a soulful liberation and education.
Like Jill Scott, I'm rhyming in similar variations… my Jill Scott,
let's take a long walk deciphering Psalms and Revelations…
…and add some poetic exegesis to all them fragmented pieces
bring some scriptural comprehension to our daughters and nieces
iron out the creases   been folded up and tucked away to long…
trying to air out all dirty laundry, shake away all that is wrong
and be strong… for Miss African American   Miss Perfect in Comparison
to all that is Perfect and Divine   Angelic features a creature so sublime
a tale for all of time   to remind   everyone of your power to
bring down showers and remove pounds of pain
make the world sound and sane…
I've wrestled with the Angel of Language to steal the right words
to express to you….   My soul's revelations.

Poetic Medicare

For you I push this pen
To befriend you with words/speak to your curves/concocting a remedy
to relax your nerves/calm the storm of a Blackwoman scorn This is why
I was born "Blackman"/thought I had no plans/but here I am
at your service, subscribing poetic prescriptions to medicate your
experience in North America back through the Middle passage –
Motherland vaccine/cocktail
the experience we've been through and seen/laced in our DNA,
the cure lies in us
it's beyond communication and trust/it's about knowing us/
us we must know to grow
beyond the pain and suffering, the lies and lust
/and this is not for pretend/not a fake
friend/but a brother from the land called Mother/Blackman from
a mad-land called ghetto, called gutter/and every word that I
utter, regardless of my stutter/is sincere/clear and simple/the
situation is beyond emotional/it's extremely mental/what I'm
speaking to, is your frame of thinking/re-framing my thinking in
alignment with yours/together, back track across the West African
shores/libation disinfecting those nasty sores/bandaged with them
garments our ancestors wore/from the heavens canopy to the ocean
floor/and everything in-between bears witness to the team we once
were we can be again and for you I push this pen, signing the
prescription for your pain/a remedy from and for the brain/polish
the stain of a grimy history/doctor your wombs with love, honesty,
respect, and add understanding to that

chemistry/speak to your spirit with passion & love, that Holy
Ministry/sustain you with loving energy/and in the end, be
your friend/remember that I push this pen for you/get well soon
I'm pushing this pen for you.

P.S. For all those sisters who love poetry.

Part IV: Embracing Love & Healing

...and there is no greater thing than this; love!

Consideration, Appreciation and all that Good Stuff

Thank You! Thank you for that sweet smile,
for showing me all of you, the adult and the child…
the grown woman and the little girl who is still growing showing
me that I'm worth your time and that your worth mine, knowing
    that I have no time to waste
patiently waiting for a taste
 a taste of you - you know what I mean… a taste of you
I'm furnishing and interior decorating a place for you
in my heart
and this is just the start
and I thank you…
thank you for every moment, I mean every single moment, the silent
moments, the loud and crazy moments, the family moments, the
laughing moments, the crying moments and every single moment
that you've opened your mouth exposed yourself in and out
the moments of truth and half-truths
the mental contradictions in your youth,
the constant intermissions waiting for God's permission
    to love you

  and I have taken nothing you do as an insult I'm an adult,
do grown man things, have grown man conversations
with grown man aspirations, but I place no expectations
on you except that you be my friend, understand me,
please comprehend, that I appreciate who you are

don’t want to change or rearrange
you, just want to embrace you,
embrace the grace in all of you
and erase any pain that men have put you
through and always be here for you
until the skies are no longer blue Thank
you, thank you for just being you

As You Are Collectively

I love this woman like I love no other/she's sister to my brother/my aunt, mother of my son/she's so young/a newborn/and old and worn/like a raisin in the sun/she's well done/finger-lickin'-good/thick thighs and breasts, they call them chickens in our hood/she's tall, she's short, the skinny, thick, slim, chubby, big-bone, flat-chested/big-breasted/dark, light-skinned/wide grin/never smile/ghetto fab, bogie style/churchgoing, thick lips/to feed her baby, says she has to strip/brown, black, and hazel eyes/tight jeans hugging those thighs/fat ass, no ass/no class/high-maintenance, professional career/short, brown, blond, maroon, Cheri-curled, extensions, weaves, dreadlocks, and long hair/long legs, slick-walking/hips talking/stretch-marked stomach, hanging breasts/cellulose and veins showing/gossiping and always knowing… somebody's business, neck-snapping/lip-smacking/child-slapping/foot tapping/hand on hip/bowlegged tight grip/pigeon-toed sister and oh how I love her… love her collectively/and I'm going to give her what she expects of me/a friend, a brother, a lover, a father/a good son who'll try harder/a real close cousin, respected neighbor/for her love I'll toil and labor/I'll be the best grandson, nephew, Uncle, grandfather, husband, and I'll deny no favor/because I love your flavors… Dark-Chocolate, Caramel, Butter Pecan, Brown Sugar, Strawberry, Vanilla, and Sweet Cinnamon/the greatest sin of men/but I'ma transcend/and treat her as the Queen/I seen/when I was born/and avoid her scorn/Celebrate her birth; baby girl/Celebrate her death; Sade girl/Celebrate her life, she made this world/from my fetus curl/to my upright position, oh how she has made this world/my baby/my lady/my shorty, old girl, sister woman, I love you so much, I truly do love you like I love no other…
sister, daughter, cousin, aunt, neighbor, grandma, niece, wife and mother.

All Sisters

I see sisters and love them all,
not the same as wanting them all, nothing like
    that… it's something like hats…
…so many flavors and styles,
fitting like an honorable crown can't smile
  at sisters without seeming to flirt
the inevitable hurt and pain
that comes with game…   no no, it's nothing like that
  it's something like hats   a closet full of designs
appreciating the interior, you know… the mind
not committing the crime   of just loving behinds,
behinds?... uh uh, it's nothing like that, that's like paying a fine,
            "Play at your own risk"
quick to get slapped, that's why sisters hands stay bent at the wrist…
…easy swing action, just like them hips
and my heart skips   a beat
when I see my sister, smell so sweet pedicure feet
Damn they can cook, damn they can eat
It's stuff like that that brings my comfort back
makes me tip my hat and clap like anchors for
more sister acts
When I say "acts" I don't mean fake pretenders
uh uh, it's nothing like that
Matter of fact I love sisters for being black
and not white, desiring slimmer hips, taller height
        thinner lips, skin that's light

no, I love them thick, love 'em slick Vaseline down
  skin that's brown   Ebonic talk, hip-swing walk
rolling eyes, bulging thighs
It's no surprise   that I love them all…
…is this man's fall
or is it man's rise it's no surprise,
I love 'em all.

(R.E.M.) No Illusion

Images are Real
And I would kill to have a dream
or fantasy with images like you dream come true
Move trough the illusion
and arrive at the substance with no intrusion
from external confusion the facts have been proven that when
I'm moving lucidly into your arms
reciprocate the embrace capture the moment before the alarm
before we awake just in time to create
an impression in the memory
So we can manifest the reality with the right chemistry…
…once we meet in real life
I've always wondered, did she dream this dream I dreamt
Where I finally said what I meant
did everything right and every moment was a blissful moment
And if you did… you never say nothing when we meet in the street
And now I seek a change an image from my dream
You said you dreamt it to an image of me and you,
where I'm faithful and true
Images are real, dreams are too
So let's dream again
We don't have to wake up, it don't have to end
So let's dream again dream again.

Love Will Heal

It's not the streets I blame
for my lust untamed   no shame
Treating love like a game
It's not the music, magazine or movies
or UV rays that got me hot
Got you saying, "Why he use me?"
It's not bad upbringing… I was raised quite good,
quiet neighborhood pretty good schooling
an okay church when my passions were repressed and my spirit was ruling,
no fooling… I wasn't always a beast in heat. My morale became weak,
spirit in defeat flesh put to the test…
…Failed… conscience put to rest
and stopped caring if you became depressed
You say no, I hear yes   You say stay for breakfast,
I got dressed and left   You look for a heart in my chest
searching for more while I settled for less
And I guess I'm the blame… now what's next?
Denial is the first sign of addiction
but now I'm admitting the problem trying to reconcile our
condition Hello, my name is Keith, and I'm a sexual addict
And I know my transformation won't be
automatic I gotta have it that's my habit
If I could rehab as a detox patient
will you put faith in me, wait a little while and be a little patient
These weaknesses and desires are old and ancient Lets blame
Adam or more so Satan the snake

ain't he a masculine figure, the father of hate,
envy, jealousy and lust, and temptation so
great Temptations that I can't shake
But I don't blame you, it's me and my own weakness and desires
Cold showers don't put out this fire
No love, just infatuation and the female body that I admire
Dire need of help I'm in, therapy, sexual discipline, hormone balance,
and a permanent cure I'll explore all remedies
Uproot these internal enemies;
lust, greed…. insensitivity, all those promiscuous deeds
and succeed… with you by my bed side, nursing me through withdrawals,
saving me from relapse,
clasp a chastity belt to my torso phallic lock-down,
my groin committed to a semen asylum,
so you and I can finally become an item,
tame my lust nurture our trust
and in the end, make amends to love, love for loving us I
know I owe you, I'm in deep debt…
Just work with me, I'll work it off in installments,
Getting through this step by step.

Secrets

Only you and God know those truths and
you've dared to share them with me,
things written in the confines of your girlhood diary…
hard-covered, locked with key… whispered over the
phone to your closest girlfriend… discussed with
your closely-held teddy bear   and you dare share them
with me… facts that are especially concealed from
your parents… and it's apparent that your openness
is beyond hopelessness… putting all trust and faith in
me see a confidant safe and secure….
Testimonies and confessions I've tried to forget, but
some truths can't be ignored… and so you dared
share them with me… the anxiety to release
the peace that another cares to share the burden burning
inside secrets to hide in me you confide, so we share a
secret you never question will I keep it, keep them…
haven't even told all to my oldest friend and I'm in…
knowing you completely, discreetly
told me the shameful, painful and most embarrassing,
balancing the good against the bad, the morals against the
desires… never doubted your truths or considered you a
liar… I admire your honesty, you've been inhaling truths
for so long that sharing has been forbidden,
concealed and hidden, written in mind and Diary
Inspired me to be just as comfortable and honest
and brave… for surely trust has been betrayed

in the past and at last we can trust each other like
lovers suppose to I'll never expose you protector of
your doubts, fears, complexes, sins, goals,
like no one knows… loose lips sink ships and
as far as that goes… don't be worried I'm
taking your secrets to the grave when I'm
dead and buried… And if someone asks I'll
lie in a hurry… no truth
even if they pulled every nail and tooth,
I'm sticking to the claim that I'm unaware,
"would she dare share, be for real"
Your deepest thoughts concealed… your
 secrets are safe with me.

False Alibi

I am afraid to lose you
Therefore I'm afraid to love you
For centuries I've been unable to protect you,
uplift you, empower you, or nourish your essence
and so I feel insufficient, inadequate, out of place,
Supplanted by a corporate society which
motivates your position and while I'm still racing
for possessions of all things material
you're racing towards fulfillment
and empowerment to be superior
that which I can't supply… and so I
lie and falsify an alibi about my
misplaced manhood, displaced
statesmanship, lost fortune
and produce an illusion of independence
and pervert your innocence your quest for completeness

To afraid to ask for your help to move beyond the
pains of a post-slavery mentality
and fashion out a future with the same sweat, blood, and
tears we've given others… to mold with our
fingerprints which are encoded with the DNA of our
ancestors…
To move onto pyramidal achievements
and beyond technology and corporate
scamming, redefine the microcosm of the family

redefining you and I… roots for nationhood,
roots for love

I'm was so afraid of losing you,
therefore I've been afraid to love you,
even though you've never left me,
despite my false alibi… *claiming manhood.*

REDUNDACY

I swear/these words that I spit will hit you right there (the heart)/my saliva moistened on that spot to show that I licked you right there/soaked through the clothing you wear caressing your mental disposition with the vocabulary used right here/moan and groan real clear/an expression signifying how I hold you so dear/so near/so many poems because I fear/that I'll lose you based on the problems we've been through this year/I've apologized for 2004 but still broke those promises that I've whispered in your ear/still hung out late, flirting and drinking beer/been talking about marriage, I'm finally ready, tell me when and where/put the past behind, forgive and forget, Abracadabra! AllaKazaam! Let it disappear/let the puppy love reappear/and I'm here/willing and ready, I swear! No more influences from my boyish peers/I swear/no more acting like I don't give a damn, I care/I swear/a wonderful life together we're going to share/I swear/I'm so sincere/I swear right now, I'm dropping tears/I swear I'm not just speaking in the air/I swear I'm trying to be with you until we die of old age in rocking chairs/you and I a pair, forever I swear/to the commandments of marriage I vow to adhere/Oh how I dare swear in the name of God, may He strike me down with a punishment that's severe/if I have an affair/I swear I'm a mamma's boy, but she won't interfere/Oh dear, Oh yeah/I'm ready, I'm here/I'll spear you all the wordplay, I'll just show you, I swear.

Size Seven

I've measured you not
with numbered tape or rulers
It was my eyes that sized…
you up for a wedding gown,
lingerie, maternity clothes, girdles,
orthopedic shoes and a burial gown
  Whether you lose or gain pounds, age
beyond age, lose sight and sound… …at
that moment I knew it was you seen
psychic visions of something old,
something borrowed, something new,
        and something blue
Love at first sight, the cliché became
        true our future in clear view
Everything Mama said you'd be like, every
imagery in my dreams and fantasies,
no flaws or fallacies…   Perfect!
I mean perfect like the sixth day of
creation I saw that it was good
Thanked and praised God for the artistic
    manifestation fulfilled all my expectations
I've measured you not with a ruler or measuring tape,
  or European dreams… of subliminal images in
        commercials and magazines
It was your skin complexion, hair, thick lips and nose,

the spirit that goes with your disposition, your pose I
measured you against my mama and every Queen
I mean… it's you I choose… for being a Black woman.

I Can Never Say It Enough

Thank you!
Thank you for your patience
for remaining high maintenance
looking your best to attract my attention
Even when I wasn't worth an honorable mention
Still cooking in the kitchen
when the atmosphere was laced with stress and tension
when I've acted like the bitch that I've often called you
and you still stuck by me after all we've gone through…
  when I had no job
when I hustled on corners
imitating the mob
When I went to the military and
went into the penitentiary
and when I eventually went to college
And I appreciate every step, every yard, every mileage…
you took to reach me to teach me
and preach to me about change,
salvation education Stock exchange
Invested in the manifested good in me, the purity,
that I collected from your reflection
a mirror of your perfection
And what you're expecting of me, I think I can accomplish
…I know I can with you holding my hand
For being dear to me,
 for being there for me… I thank you!

A Self-Esteem Enhancer

Self-conscious about your curves… so you diet
Can't control your nerves… they run a riot
…so you smoke
Can't find a man that winds his hips and grinds so you settle
for a man that pokes
It's the murder she wrote I'm taking notes,
diagnosing the symptoms and prescribing the remedy,
so you'll stop sleeping with the enemy… …like
BODYGUARD Life is hard enough
with that white stuff intoxicating your mind
hating the shape of your behind Got
magazine image syndrome,
so you frequent spots where white men roam
Enduring dis-ease just to be pleased
You say that you're only with our adversary,
for a moment that is temporary
You say a man is a man, sex is sex, pleasure is
pleasure, despite his short measure
And it's those images of Barbie and Kenny,
that has you all skinny, sipping on Martin, Remy,
guzzling that "slim is in" propaganda
Why can't you stay thick like Ms. Lewis, Ananda
and stay black like a panther
Let Blackmen love you like a hip-hop R&B summer anthem
Yes, indeed, I'll be your answer, when you're ready to come back
from the back I'll be your breast and rump enhancer

Yes, I love your dark skin and all your curves,
expressing it best with poetic words
So love yourself, like I love you Sis…
Let my love be the remedy and we'll get through this.

Damage Control

Just call me Mr. Fix It, Mr. Make It Right and invite me into your existence, because I want to re-maintenance you; high maintenance sister, and dig deep into your soul and offer you closure from the rot and the mold… from the exposure of dis-eased thinking individuals, and heal you whole… this is my mission…kissing your wounds and scars and re-highlight the stars in your eyes and make them shine brighter than they already do
and readjust your bones so you can stand taller, more erect, more perfect than before, more sure of your divine nature. And I want to put you in a hypnotic trance, make you remember that in every bad experience you still came out the victor, stronger, sharper, brighter and more refined …. unaffected by the damage of time… disregard the pain and embrace what came next… walking away every time with answers… and I want to help you apply the right answers… use every remedy to remove them emotional cancers… be your private doctor, your private dancer… and dance into your soul, letting the rhythm of love ballads unfold… and slow dance with your heart and jump start your sweet soul and cause you to feel as if you've never been hurt… love is hard work… and I'll get my hands dirty, if you deem me to be worthy… and I'm pulling out all the equipment, all my expensive tools to use on every bone that's been bruised… and tighten you up with my liquid screws, you know, like how the tongue ring moves…. I have to take that invention from that white guy, he just trying to get his groove on, I'm trying to take you on a lifetime cruise… I want to eroticize your mind first, fulfill your spirits thirst and burst through your flesh with a sanitized needle… and inject in you everything that the soul needs and feed you… wisdom, respect, power, understanding, life, love and all the above.

No More Disrespect

From now on she shall be respected and held
high extolled beyond the sky
Stevie called her "the apple of my eyes"
and I cry… tears of joy
exposing the man-child's inner-boy
employ the respect of all my brothers
grandmothers are the best huggers
and this is where I place my face
in that bosom cushioned warm embrace
and trace our roots…
…I'm talking about that Alex Haley
tracing racing back to the Motherland
where we held our Mother's hand
from our birth until our death…
she carried the load in her belly, on her head,
in arms, six pounds sucking from her breast…
and you're at your best
when we're at our worse… when you've reversed roles
and have been our Fathers and masculine role models
nursed us from the bottle… and here's where my pride gets swallowed,
rejuvenated into pride for you… held high in view,
of all your accomplishments; much respect due…
No more disrespect, in honor of you.

Preview of: "The Redemption"

(No Titles)

Playing Safe House:
She dried humped me unto her wetness
No intercourse, just a dry rub
as her bush scrubbed
against my rushing blood
and we exploded like light bulbs with an idea
No fear of pregnancy or STD's
sexing like virgins
before the innocence is lost
at the cost of curiosity....an overrated discovery
Consideration, Generosity.....and we thanked one another.

*

To many times
Made the bed rock
Out of wedlock
Like Russian roulette

dodged another bullet

(Whew)

#BillyJean

Thankful that it's a life

And not death

Unprotected

But God Protected

That child is Blessed...

Happy I am I guess

She said my heart was cold like Ice/that some days I'm manly other days I roll with the mice/get drunk like I'm high/chinky eye /chicken and rice/we all have a vice a poison/enjoying shit that kills us/and what's real love without real trust/we men wishing that women could feel us/women feeling like we only have a will to buss/we scream and cuss/fight and fuss and when the dust clears/no one hears the other person/because of the cursing/the curse within the Karma/ have to walk around with Voodoo doll armor/because Even though I don't mean to harm her/she spitefully will hurt me/a woman scorn will hurt me. But though I'm a sinner, The Lord won't desert me/those who are blessed can't be curse/pay attention to this verse/those who are blessed can't be cursed....armored by the Holy Spirit/the Word I can hear it/come close, get near it/heaven is calling the man that has fallen/Was crawling and now asks for forgiveness/Back straight, standing tall, this is repentance/return of the innocence/we all can start fresh/and

so I stop being fresh/not concerned with being
fly/getting drunk, getting high/getting over or getting by/and definitely
being mindful not to make her cry...because I want to die in peace.
All I want to do is die in peace.
And she Is Peace.

She has cheek bones
Like Nefertiti's throne
A smile like the Ivory Coast
bright like the sunshine,
Full of hope
A face full of grace
and beauty that
encompasses the
distance between her and I
Which is how I see her in the
clouds, see her in the sky
See her in my dreams
See her in my mind
So sweet, so fine, divine like
Plays the background
Never in the limelight
but shines brighter than the rest
Long beautiful legs, nice chest
And she makes me lose my breath
Brings the noise makes me lose my breath

Hits me hard
makes me lose my breath
(hah hah)
Her natural beauty
and natural hair....
Her delicate touch
and innocent stare....
And I dare
Love to love her
because I trust her heart
trust her intellect
I know that she's smart
the lust comes after the respect
And I know this is the start
of something beautiful
If you're
Reading this
It's too late
Have my heart for life
Friend or wife
BFF sounds nice
because when true
friendship is the root
no one gets the boot
And love is everlasting
Not just a passion
that's passing through

But something real
Something true
I love you

*

I Adore You
I knew it from the first touch/
that what we would have would be so much....more
than a quick score/that we would explore
the idea/of loving without fear.....recklessly.
I knew from the first kiss
That this.....was a fulfillment of a prayer and a wish
Born from tears that
are now dismissed unless accompanied by bliss.
I knew from the start that I had met my Isis/
that you'd heal my emotional crisis/ and that we would
together embrace the things that have no prices......like time,
knowledge, spirituality, Truth and Love.
I knew from the first ride/that I could die/within your bosom,
but would rather live within your heart/until death do us apart.....
......I knew from the start/that it may all seem premature/
and we may need more time to explore/offer more in order to be sure/
before using the 3 words that describe Amore.......
but the emotion and energy is so raw, so pure,
so divine/that it became a must that I claimed you as mine/
and allow you to claim me as yours......
.....I'm so sure
I Adore You.

Southern Sexuality:
She was curvy like
Turkey Neck Bones
Smothered in Lust

*

I think she sprinkles a little something addictive in her draws/Like cocaine raw/has me breaking many laws/to get more/its the Murder she wrote/the murder I saw/.....

What?!
You have no baggage?
Then let me toss my trunk.
Come hop on this bus
and let's discuss...
Our future

The End

The Beginning

To Be Continued

.

P.S. To the Brown-skin girls who idolize Marilyn Monroe
That Bitch was trash....a slut...a whore.....a hoe
And she idolized you
Amen

Notes

About The Author

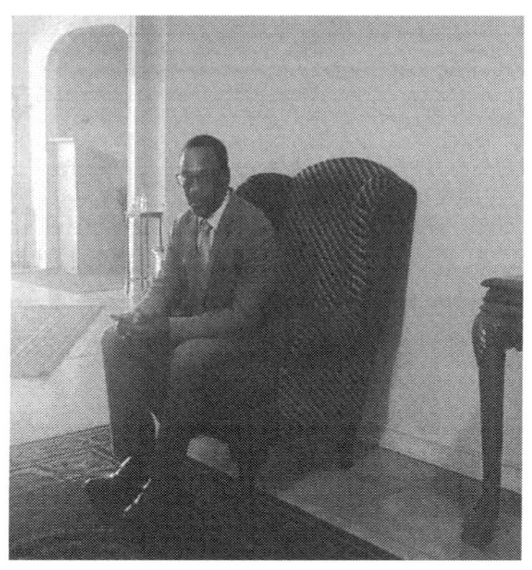

***E**luhim Barraq - Siddha (Royal Melvin Warren Jr.) is from Brooklyn, New York. He has authored the collection of poems titled "The Apology: A Blackman's Contrition to His Sisters", which is his first book. The poems in this book are poems that address the joys and accomplishments as well as the pains and struggles of black women throughout the world. These poems highlight women's impact on the world, in our lives and adds another voice to her-story.*

Eluhim was raised by a hard working religious mother who instilled in him the principle of what it means to value and respect a woman in action and in word. The village that raised Eluhim also consisted of grandparents, Aunts, uncles, step-family, teachers and neighbors that all contributed to his understanding of this universal truth that; "women are the cradle of civilization, without them we would not be".

Currently blessing the spoken word circuit Eluhim divides his time between New York, Maryland and the Carolinas stepping on stages and holding Poetry Over Dinner events in homes where the setting and discussions about his poems are more intimate. He also creates events for other artists to be heard and recognized. During his travels he is also working on his third book of poetry, and a motivational book for young men while at the same time doing his best to evolve into the man that his village raised him to be; that being, a better son, brother, nephew, uncle, father and husband. Eluhim often says, "My greatest aspiration is to be a man and let no one and nothing remove me from that position".

Contact for Book Signings, Readings, Discussion Events and Performances @
rmelwarren@gmail.com
https://www.facebook.com/eluhim.siddha?ref=tn_tnmn
www.facebook.com/theapology77
https://www.instagram.com/p/SdcnDelCgJ/?

Made in the USA
Columbia, SC
25 June 2021